"This book can help anyone learn to be a better swimmer, regardless of ability. Terry Laughlin's explanation of proper technique and his unique system for practicing it will help anyone swim better. He easily makes an improved stroke simple for the novice, yet I've seen his methods work for elite swimmers too."

—David Marsh, 1996 United States Olympic Team Coach;
Head Coach, Auburn University

"Terry Laughlin is the 90s innovator on how to swim correctly. His approach to teaching swimming is well-thought-out, precisely methodical, and he has been able to I.D. the three key elements to better swimming no matter your skill level. I have witnessed it work!"

—Gerry Rodrigues, Publisher of *SWIM* magazine;
Masters World Champion; Head Coach of UCLA Masters

"The most valuable service a good coach provides is to sharpen your stroke technique, not make you work harder. Terry Laughlin has done an outstanding job of simplifying that complex subject, providing practical tools that will let anyone be his or her own best coach."

—Eddie Reese, United States Olympic Team Coach 1992 and 1996;
Head Coach NCAA Champion University of Texas

"Finally! For over four years I've been looking for ways to get faster in the water by coaching myself. In just two days of Total Immersion training I learned enough to change the way I think about swimming. Terry Laughlin actually taught me how to teach myself. And whenever I need a refresher, the skills for that are right at my fingertips too."

—Mike Pigg, World Champion Triathlete

"*Total Immersion* will do more to improve your triathlon performance than any other coaching or training method."

—*Triathlete* magazine

"This book is a wonderful contribution to swimming. I am so impressed that I shall immediately be distributing it to my swim school teachers and coaches."

—Forbes Carlile, M.B.E., M.Sc., Australian Olympic Team Coach;
Director, Carlile Swimming Organization

"How many people can say that they swam around Manhattan—28.5 miles—and had fun doing it? Thank you so much for helping to make my marathon swim such a memorable experience. I'll tell anyone who is serious about improving their swimming that *Total Immersion* is the answer."

—Don Walsh

"Your instruction has made a radical difference in my fitness swimming. Swimming has gone from one more thing to check off my list to one of the most rewarding parts of my day."

—Jenny Frederick

". . . I learned more about swimming fast with less effort than I have during thirty years of competitive and Masters swimming. I'd recommend *Total Immersion* to anyone wanting to swim better or faster regardless of their swimming backround."

—Bill Geiser

"Thanks for a great learning experience. Terry Laughlin is an excellent teacher with a masterful understanding of the interconnection between mind and muscle. I got exactly what I needed to become a better swimmer."

—Joe Neri

"My friends can't believe how much I improved . . . I've already taken an amazing 40 seconds off my best time for 800 meters!"

—Joanne Lazzaro

Total Immersion

The Revolutionary Way to Swim Better, Faster, and Easier

Terry Laughlin
with John Delves

A Fireside Book
Published by Simon & Schuster

FIRESIDE
Rockefeller Center
1230 Avenue of the Americas
New York, NY 10020

FIRESIDE and colophon are registered trademarks
of Simon & Schuster Inc.

Designed by Elina Nudelman

Manufactured in the United States of America

10   9   8   7   6   5   4

Library of Congress Cataloging-in-Publication Data
Laughlin, Terry.
    Total immersion : the revolutionary way to swim better, faster, and easier / Terry
Laughlin with John Delves.
        p.   cm.
    "A Fireside book."
    Includes index.
    (alk. paper)
    1. Swimming—Training.   I. Delves, John.   II. Title.
GV837.7.L38   1996
797.2'1—dc20   96-15772
                                                                                CIP

ISBN 0-684-81885-X

I dedicate this book to three gentlemen from
the world of swimming who enriched my life beyond measure:

To coach Dick Krempecki, who coached me at St. John's University,
who inspired me to want to be a swimming coach.

To coach Bill Irwin, who coached me at Manhasset Swim Club,
who inspired me to be a swimming coach who teaches.

To coach Bill Boomer, who opened my eyes
to a whole new way of teaching.

ACKNOWLEDGMENTS

With a busy schedule of workshops to teach and a business to run, I could never have found the time to write this book without the invaluable assistance of numerous people who deserve my thanks: John Delves, since 1990 my most valued editor and friend as well, for turning some great thoughts on swimming into a great read. My brother, Steve Laughlin, for turning words about swimming drills into pictures that anyone can follow. My friends and colleagues, Denise Ullrich and David Cohen, who run the operational side of Total Immersion, allowing me to put all of my energies into coaching and writing about swimming. My daughters, Fiona, Cari, and Betsy, for sharing their dad with swimmers all over America each weekend. To my editor at Simon & Schuster, Becky Cabaza, whose enthusiasms for swimming and for the printed word, not to mention her patience, were the perfect combination of qualities for this project. And finally, to my wife and partner, Alice, for urging me to commit my ideas to paper, for organizing my life and providing as much support as any swimming coach has ever received.

CONTENTS

— — — — — — — — — — — — — — — — — — **Contents**

Contents — — — — — — — — — — — — — —

INTRODUCTION

You are about to begin an adventure that, like all adventures, is going to change you a little. It will, that is, as long as you can keep yourself open-minded enough to give new ideas a chance. If you can, all the way through this book, I promise that by the end, you'll no longer think of water and swimming the way you used to. You'll understand what good swimming is *really* about, and just how you can achieve it for yourself.

It doesn't matter if you're brand-new to the sport, a regular looking around for tips on how to improve, or a frustrated "old-timer" who's "known it all" for years but still can't seem to squeeze any more speed out of that stroke of yours. *Total Immersion: The Revolutionary Way to Swim Better, Easier, and Faster* is a better-swimming game plan for all adults, from lap and fitness swimmers to triathletes and former college competitors who once lived, breathed, ate, and slept the sport. The Total Immersion self-help program will do nothing less than give you all the tools you need to be your own best coach, no matter who you are, no matter how well you currently swim. And I can promise that you'll come to enjoy the sport more than you ever have before.

Everyone knows swimming is the most nearly perfect exercise, whether you're in your teens, 20s, 30s, or—especially—in middle age and beyond. It's a great workout that's easy on the joints.

But there's a discouraging myth about swimming too, the myth that you have to plod through thousands of boring laps to be any good; "following the black line," it's called with a fatalistic shrug. It's a fiction that discourages people from getting into the pool and enjoying themselves. Just as bad, it also prevents swimmers already there from becoming far better. Small wonder that although 80 million Americans consider swimming their favorite form of exercise, according to *Swimming World* magazine, few ever swim well enough to become fit. The American Swimming Coaches Association and the National Swim School Association both estimate that only 2 percent of all Americans can swim a quarter-mile without stopping. That's not a random distance, unfortunately. It's the minimum for a decent aerobic workout.

Total Immersion can change that. Following the black line is out. Learning and practicing are in. This book will show you how to swim better and enjoy your pool time far more, using the techniques I've developed during 30 years of coaching and swimming. My method is unlike anyone else's, and this book is too. *Total Immersion* will change the very way you think of your body as it moves through water, whether for fun or for exercise.

The core of the program is this: The body struggles to learn complicated motions—like a fluid and powerful swim stroke. But it easily masters the simple ones into which every complicated motion can be broken. So in the Total Immersion program, you start from the ground up, gradually and easily assembling all the parts of an improved stroke using the unique, "bite-size" skill drills. Then, since the body can faithfully do what "feels right" as long as it knows what that is, I have designed what I call sensory skill practice. It makes correct swimming instinctive and intuitive instead of something you have to constantly think about and labor over.

Use this book the same way. It will work most effectively for you if you read the whole thing first, to see how the pieces of this novel puzzle gradually fit together and what each one will do for you. But chances are you won't want to wait that long to get started, especially when you see how thoroughly each simple step is explained and how easy it is to master. If you'd prefer to "swim while you study," that's fine too. Here's the best way to make the book work for you that way.

Part One, Chapters 1 to 8, is the core of the better-swimming techniques I teach at my Total Immersion workshops. You'll first learn why swimming lap after lap has done you frustratingly little good, and what you'll now do instead. Subsequent chapters show you why the *position of your body,* not the *pull of your arms,* is the key to swimming better fast, and how you can become balanced and "slippery." Once you've finished Chapter 3, try the simple "drag-eliminating" exercises a couple of times and watch what happens. These body-streamlining exercises are the foundation of everything to come. And as unconventional as it all seems at first, the proof is there, based on principles of ship design and everyday physics that have somehow never before been applied to swimming instruction.

Skill drills, the step-by-step core of the Total Immersion learning process, come next. They're so simple to explain that you could skip to Chapter 8 and start doing them right away, but they'll mean more —and probably work faster for you—if you understand *why* they work, what they feel like when they are working properly, and how you'll gradually integrate them into your regular swimming, covered in Chapters 4 through 7.

Chapter 8 is where we officially leave the classroom behind and start developing the individual bite-size movements that will ultimately be put together into your new, smoother swim stroke. It's organized logically into four lessons, each of which builds on the one before. It's important to do them in order, but the pace is yours. Don't move on to the next lesson until you're completely comfortable with the one you've been working on. When you've finished each lesson, go back to Chapters 6 and 7 for the drill-swim and sensory skill practices that will make what you've practiced a permanent part of your stroke. You'll find a sample, step-by-step plan for going about this in the appendix.

Now that you're swimming a new way, you should train differently too. So Part Two explains how and why, proving the Total Immersion principle that "fitness is something that happens to you while you're practicing good technique." You'll see that, from now on, moving right always comes before muscle power. And you'll get better results from the time you have to spend in the pool. You'll enjoy it far more too.

With the theory and practice of the Total Immersion program under your belt, you're ready to face the future. Swimming right is something most people want to enjoy for a long, long time, and the advice in Part Three on strength training, weight loss, and injury prevention will help make that possible. So will the exciting possibilities for doing things you may never have tried—from making new friends by joining U.S. Masters Swimming to "racing" a postal meet where you mail in your times.

The message is simple. Forget everything you've heard about swimming. What you "know" is *wrong*. It is too complicated, difficult to follow, frustrating, and, worst of all, probably wastes your energy and time concentrating on the wrong things. To become a good swimmer you need neither brawn nor youth, great athleticism nor impressive endurance. You need skill, and you need smart training. With this book as your swim partner, you will have both.

PART ONE

New Moves:
Teaching Yourself to Swim a Whole New Way

Chapter 1

Swimming Laps and Going Nowhere

It's no mystery why people have trouble swimming as fast or as far or as smoothly as they'd like—most of them are doing it backward. "Don't worry if your form's not perfect," coaches and instructors have always assured us. "Just get those laps in. Eventually, you'll be fit enough to develop a smoother, stronger stroke." It really works the other way around, but that's not how it's been taught.

Until now. Let me tell you how I came to discover what good swimming is *really* all about, and what this means to anyone who would rather spend his or her time growing faster and smoother instead of just growing tired—and who wants to do it all as quickly as possible.

But first, a confession. I'm addicted to the sport of swimming. I leave my house at 6:00 most mornings to keep my daily swimming "appointment," I compete in meets whenever I can, and, last but not least, I earn my living teaching other adults how to become addicted too.

Hard to imagine it any other way because, in my opinion, swimming is more fun than anything else you can do with your clothes on. It feels great and, no matter how hard the workout, you're left so refreshed, so energized, that for the rest of the day no challenge seems too great.

Name one other workout that can do that. After running, I ache all day long and often into the next. Cycling is fun and is certainly fine exercise, but only as long as the sun's up and it's not cold or wet out. Weight training is excellent, but by the time I'm done, it's all I can do to carry my gym bag back to the car.

Swimming's different. I always feel better after my workout than I did before. That's what makes it so easy to leave a comfortable bed even before sunup on a frosty morning, or on a sultry summer predawn, to get to the pool on time.

Perhaps calling swimming "the ideal exercise" is a little strong, but it would be hard to find a better contender for the title. It makes your heart and lungs work more efficiently, enhances muscle strength and endurance, improves flexibility, and helps reduce stress. Yet swimming is easier on the joints than anything else that gets your heart rate up. Unless you count cross-country skiing, swimming uses more muscles than all other exercises. And it's the only one that can legitimately make you feel weightless and free.

Tired of the battle scars of other aerobic sports? Swimming is about as injury-free as they come. Gone are the bone-jarring shocks of land sports, so gone too are the joint and back injuries that plague so many joggers and cyclists. The water is also kinder to your muscles. Its massaging effect and the steady, even resistance it provides eliminate much of the postworkout muscle soreness so common in land sports.

Overheating is also nearly impossible in swimming. Water conducts heat from the body 20 times better than air does, so you can train at much higher intensities—in summer particularly—without the dehydration and potential heat exhaustion common "ashore."

And swimming is an equal-opportunity sport. Even if your weight, a physical handicap, or an injury would normally keep you out of action on land, you can probably swim. In fact, many land athletes use swimming to regain strength and fitness after an injury, far sooner than they could by returning to their main sport.

Joints growing stiffer with time? One of the most important reasons for an adult to swim is to increase flexibility, because this sport promotes joint mobility better than any other aerobic exercise. And while swimming's no fountain of cardiological youth, a 1988 study by cardiologists and exercise physiologists at the University of Texas Health Science Center in Dallas showed that inactive adults improved their heart function significantly within just three months of beginning a swim-training program. Their hearts beat more slowly and powerfully and circulated blood more effectively. Regular swimmers have also been shown to have lower blood pressures, slower pulse rates, and much greater exercise tolerance than other people their age. On top of all this, the aerobic benefits of swimming one mile are equal to those of running four miles.

None of this mattered—since little of it was known anyway—when I swam in college. Swim training was simple then: You stepped up and took your medicine. Take enough of it as often as possible, and you'd win the race you were training for. It was *supposed* to hurt, or you had no business calling yourself a competitive swimmer. And who could ask questions when your heart was always pounding and your muscles never stopped aching?

But the time for questions was coming, and it finally started during a 20-year coaching stint after college. At last, I could watch other swimmers from the pool deck as only a coach can. What an eye-opener! I finally realized that somehow, for some reason, a gifted few were able to swim extremely well without even breathing hard. It turned out to be no illusion. During some personal coaching, I was astounded to find they could, in fact, swim that well with comparatively little effort. And apparently it was that efficiency, not any unusual capacity for grueling work, that kept them consistently ahead of their competitors.

Was this an inbred gift or could it be taught, I wondered. Too soon to know for sure, but the signs were already there. Time after time, average swimmers would suddenly start improving when I stopped them from doing nothing but beating themselves up with hard training and started them on drills and exercises that let them use their existing power better.

Truth to tell, I enjoyed "cheating the system." By teaching my ath-

Swimming Laps and Going Nowhere — — — — — — — ☐

letes to be more efficient than their rivals, I gave them an edge they could use to outperform swimmers who trained for many more hours —all of which saved me a lot of time on deck. Let's be honest: Even a dedicated swim coach doesn't relish countless hours watching people grind out endless laps. And as I became a "stroke teacher" more than a workout monitor, I no longer had to.

Then, in 1988, everything began to fall into place and the real secrets of successful swimming became more obvious. That was the fateful year I met Bill Boomer and subsequently left college coaching to work exclusively with adults. Boomer, whom I refer to so often in my workshops that some campers probably think they've met him, was swimming coach at the University of Rochester in upstate New York. Though relatively unknown in the wider world of American swimming, Boomer had a cult following among other college coaches in the region, coaches whose teams regularly faced his—and not often successfully. His ideas about swimming were considered radical, even revolutionary, and obviously worth listening to.

One memorable day, Boomer addressed a coaches' clinic I happened to be attending. Speaker after speaker had gone on and on about how they trained their swimmers by "building the engine and fuel tank," so to speak—throwing enough hard work at them that their bodies had no choice but to build endurance.

Then Boomer took the podium and dropped his bomb. He posed an obvious question, but one I'd never heard in two decades of attending such meetings: "How can we teach people to swim, at any given speed, *with less effort?*" His answer was just as disarming, and just as radical: "By reshaping the vessel." After all, swimmers had a lot in common with boats, and like a naval architect Boomer knew there were ways to improve the efficiency of their "hull designs."

Detroit had been doing it with cars since the price of fuel shot out of sight in the early 1970s, but no one, until Boomer, had thought of visualizing swimming the same way. Apparently he simply had the advantage of fresh eyes and an open mind, since he hadn't even been a swimmer himself, studying movement science in school and coaching soccer and track. So Boomer came to swimming minus the usual baggage of how things "ought" to be done and with a deep understanding of the way the human body moves. That enabled him to see things the rest of us had missed.

Boomer didn't have to tell me twice. I knew right away that he was onto something, and working exclusively with adults gave me the unique opportunity to test it, develop it, and refine it. My Total Immersion workshops began concentrating on something no other swim coach in America had ever done: teaching swimming *technique* instead of giving workouts. In a sense, I was becoming more like a golf or tennis pro than a workout planner.

And the adult swimmers I was already specializing in were the ideal athletes to develop this with. As my training program grew far more sophisticated than just "more laps, more laps" and essentially became a program of precise technique, I had to make advanced skills easy to practice for older swimmers, most of whom had little experience in the sport and little understanding of what really made them move in the pool. None of us would get anywhere unless I figured out a way to distill relatively complex and advanced ideas into a series of simple, logical practice exercises that anyone could do. And since I had to travel to pools all over the U.S. each week, teaching a new group of students every time in just a few short days, the program had to be easily understood, quickly absorbed, and simple to practice after I was gone.

That was thousands of swimmers ago. Over the last few years my students have also been my partners in a long-running laboratory, making clear which instructions were too hard to understand or produced negligible results, helping me refine the ones that showed the most promise, and always being part of the search for a better, simpler, more direct route to better swimming.

Along the way, I learned that the usual "swim-your-laps" advice was not only ineffective; it could actually be harmful. If your form is making swimming difficult for you and you practice that form over and over, "following the black line," it's going to become more than bad form. It will become a bad habit. A hard-to-break one too, when you finally decide to.

Today, there's no question that swimming cannot be thoroughly understood nor effectively taught unless it's seen for what it is: primarily a skill sport like golf, tennis, or even skiing, rather than a power or endurance sport like running or cycling. And harder yet for people to accept is the fact that your skill is far more powerfully influenced by how you position and move your torso, or core, than by what you do with your arms and legs. Fanciful theory? Not at all. As you'll see later on in this book, the world's top swimming scientists have only lately discovered this to be true as they studied how world-record-holders swim.

A beautifully efficient stroke and the effortless swimming it makes possible are not prizes reserved for the lucky few who got them as gifts of nature or spent most of their waking adolescent hours grooming them. They can be taught. Contrary to much of the swimming advice you still hear, great technique is not an asset that carries a staggering price.

Lou Fiorina, an exceptional teacher who often coaches with me at Total Immersion workshops, knows that now. But he didn't always. Fiorina remembers that when he watched Rowdy Gaines and Tracy Caulkins, both legends of American swimming, putting on a demonstration at a children's clinic several years ago, he thought, "They're so fluid and graceful moving up and down the pool. You must have to be amazingly gifted to swim like that." Some months later, he went to another clinic. This time Bill Boomer was teaching a group of average college swimmers, and Fiorina was astounded by what was going on. "As I watched, I could see their strokes begin to show a lot of the same grace and elegance [as those of Gaines and Caulkins], and I suddenly realized that this stuff was *teachable,* that ordinary swimmers could learn to swim like elite athletes, and they could learn it fairly quickly."

Today they are doing just that, at Total Immersion swim camps using the exact principles you'll learn in this book, principles that are easily mastered by swimmers of any age. I've seen athletes in their 70s and 80s use these principles to improve their swim times and their fitness, *and* get the best possible workout in the bargain—doubling the payback from their pool time. The techniques are captured in a set of simple-to-learn skill drills, sequenced into a self-taught system different from anything you'll find anyplace else. Even athletes proficient in other sports but inexperienced as swimmers have learned to swim with an amazing degree of efficiency and beauty. This program can make any swimmer his or her own best coach.

Every minute of Total Immersion pool time is devoted to building proper technique, not by grinding out more and harder laps but by concentrating on fewer, easier, and more purposeful laps—stopping time-wasting "workouts" and focusing on efficient and effective "practice." Today, most swimmers who come to a Total Immersion workshop have been swimming for months or even years without seeing any progress. I hope I don't sound like a carnival barker when I tell you that when they learn the Total Immersion method, they begin to feel better and see improvement in their swimming almost immediately. You can too.

Where do the workouts go? Oh, you'll eventually do some speed and stamina training, but in the beginning at least, your fitness is an automatic dividend of skill-building. If you want to improve your tennis game, do you spend 40 minutes running back and forth between the baselines, getting in shape to chase shots? Not likely. You improve your tennis game by practicing your stroke for 40 or 45 minutes and, as you improve your game, you build the fitness you need to play tennis. We do the same thing in the pool, which is why I always open Total Immersion workshops with what I hope is welcome news to time-starved swimmers: *"Here, fitness is something that happens to you while you practice good technique."*

That's not just good news, it's good science. We now know that while conditioning matters, it doesn't matter nearly as much as we've been told. In fact, the world's top researchers estimate that champion swimmers owe about 70 percent of their great performance to perfect stroke mechanics and only around 30 percent to their fitness—a statistic you'll meet again and again in this book as we develop your new Total Immersion coaching strategy. For the rest of us "non-champs," stroke efficiency is even more crucial, controlling perhaps 90 percent of our performance. Think about it. A new swimmer who does a quarter-mile in ten minutes might shave five or ten seconds by whipping himself into better shape. But he could lop off a healthy 50 to 55 seconds simply by learning how to move more efficiently through the water.

Make no mistake: A good, efficient swimming stroke is one of life's more complicated skills, far more difficult to perfect than the ideal golf swing or the picture-perfect tennis serve. You can't come close without some expert instruction. But good teachers for adults have been hard to find, teachers who don't drown you in such a baffling sea of detail on how to move your arm every inch of the way that you forget which arm you're moving in the first place.

Worse yet, your armstroke actually has a very limited impact on how fast you move through the water. Take a horribly inefficient one and make it nearly perfect, and you might eke out a 5 or 10 percent increase in speed. That's because water is 1,000 times denser than air and throws huge drag forces against anyone who doesn't know the tricks of becoming slippery. Learning to cut that drag by improving your body position could well give you a 20 to 30 percent speed boost in just a day or two. It happens all the time at Total Immersion weekend workshops.

That's why we teach swimming "from the inside-out," just the way you'll learn it in this book. First, we show you how to get the body balanced, streamlined, and stabilized. Then, we get to work on your propulsion system—but only the parts that matter.

This way opens a world of new rewards. With your body working as it was meant to, swimming becomes a pleasure all by itself, not just an exercise or a sport to compete in. And when you concentrate on form, which is the key to this program, you will not only become fit and efficient, you'll find yourself developing an inner focus, like students of Yoga or Tai Chi.

Grace, speed, technical proficiency, fitness, *and* peace of mind. Wait a minute—is this a swimming book or a whole human potential movement? You'll find the answer in the following pages, so let's get started. It's swimming we're going to be talking about, and you've no time to be skeptical. You've got more important things to do.

Swimming Laps and Going Nowhere — — — — — — — — —

Chapter 2

Swim Better Without Getting Any Stronger? Yes!

I wasn't always smart about swimming. In fact, like most everyone who competed in college, I spent four years doing it all wrong—though nobody realized it was wrong back then. No pain, no gain, we were warned. So hour after wearying hour, we put up with the pain. Some of us got results; many of us got more than a little frustrated from time to time. The problem was simple: We were working very hard to accomplish the wrong things. And to this day, too many people are still putting themselves through that dead-end kind of drudgery.

It happened like this. Early in my freshman season—still a stranger to serious daily training—I was timed for my first 1650 ever, swimming's so-called "metric mile." It took me about 22 minutes. The top swimmers in our conference were a good four minutes faster, so if I wanted to

get anywhere in distance swimming, I had my work cut out for me. And the only way I could figure out to do that was to speed up my stroke—exactly what most improvement-minded swimmers think even today. Hands move faster, body goes faster. What could be simpler? Besides, nobody bothered to disagree.

So each afternoon, my practice strategy was as simple as it gets: Move the arms as fast as I could for as long as I could. Makes you tired in a hurry, I quickly found out, but I figured that by doing it every day I'd get used to it—you know, teach my body to laugh at fatigue. And there was a certain medieval logic to it anyway. After diving into this punishment for two hours and 240 laps every afternoon in practice, race day felt like a breeze. It was over in under 20 minutes and 66 laps. What a snap! Call it primitive sport psychology, but I hadn't a doubt in the world I was doing the right thing.

And sure enough, within two years I had achieved my goal: swimming 18 minutes, to score in the Eastern Collegiate Championships. Victory! As I dragged myself out of the pool after finishing, the timer in my lane exclaimed, "I've never seen anyone move their arms that fast for that long!"

"Thanks," I muttered.

Neither of us understood at the time that it was not a compliment.

But I eventually found out. Because even though at that point I'd been training seriously for only two years, I never swam any faster. I had wrung all the potential out of my strategy. There was noplace else to find more speed.

Though I didn't realize it at the time—still doggedly determined to find some way to work harder yet—I had crashed into the limits of the most basic rule that governs how you produce swimming speed: $V = SL \times SR$. Velocity (V) is a product of how far you travel on each stroke (stroke length or SL) multiplied by how fast you take each stroke (stroke rate or SR). As you begin to approach the upper limits of how quickly you can move your arms, you can usually speed them up even more only by decreasing your stroke length. So it's a zero-sum game. Increase one and decrease the other by the same amount and your product—velocity—doesn't budge. Worse yet, you're burning up much more energy to achieve nothing. During my final two years of hard work in college, I perfected that frustrating formula.

But all that was about to change. The summer after graduation, I took my first coaching job. Finally I could analyze swimming from a comfortable position on the deck, a vastly improved perspective to determine what makes people fast in the water over what I'd had as a swimmer, frothing up and down the pool in a haze of pain. And from day one, it struck me plain as day: The fastest swimmers made it look the easiest.

The eggbeaters churning busily were all in the slower lanes, struggling in the wake of people who seemed to glide almost casually up and down. Could I have actually looked like those ineffectual water choppers? No doubt. So I staked out my first mission as a coach: to save my swimmers from repeating my mistakes. Instead of simply driving them to work as hard as possible, I would try to figure out what allowed my best swimmers to make it look so easy, then teach it to everyone else.

I operated on that instinct for the next 12 years, and it worked. Then, in 1984, we began to find out why. In a study conducted at the U.S. Olympic Swimming Trials, Bill Boomer and some sports science colleagues from the University of Rochester filmed every length swum by every swimmer in 26 men's and women's events over six days, a total of more than 700 demonstrations by some of the world's best of how to swim as fast as a human can.

Over and over, what they found was that long event or short, *the fastest swimmers took the fewest strokes.* And it was no fluke. Four years later, a similar study by Penn State researchers at the 1988 Olympics produced the same result. The swiftest swimmers were always the most efficient.

So how could anyone learn to swim better and faster? We now had the answer: Work on longer, not faster, strokes. In my own practices today a quarter-century removed from the disappointments of my college days, that's why I care less how many yards I total than about *how many yards I travel on each stroke.* And that's why I never judge myself just by the pace clock when I'm trying to swim faster. Instead, I also measure how many additional strokes I need to gain that speed. In other words, what's it costing me?

So goal one for anyone who would swim better and faster is a longer stroke. This can happen in two ways: 1. more push—using your hands and feet to *thrust* your body farther through the water by making each stroke as powerful as possible, and 2. less drag—shaping your body so it's more friction-free, allowing it to travel farther with the power each of your strokes is already producing.

Of course, in the water your instincts "know" just what to do. Pull harder, kick harder, spin your arms faster. All wrong, of course. That's how I squandered four years of college swimming. Too bad I didn't know then what 25 years of coaching has taught me about how the world's best swimmers actually produce *their* speed. Most of it comes from how well they shape and position their bodies to eliminate drag and become more "slippery"—relatively little from how they use their hands and arms to push the water around.

A freestyler sprinting at world-record pace puts out over a thousand watts of power to "streak" down the pool at a paltry five mph. Yet fish have been clocked at 68 mph—as fast as a cheetah can run—with amazingly little energy expenditure. A 100-ton blue whale, cruising at 20 mph, should require some 448 horsepower, according to the calculations of Georgia Tech physics professor Vincent Mallette, but in fact gets by with fewer than 70. A dolphin also uses only about one-eighth the power that simple physics says it should.

The human being, land-adapted for millions of years, struggles awkwardly when trying to propel himself through a substance 1,000 times denser than air. Every movement is bought at an extravagant cost in energy. To double speed in the water requires eight times as much power output. To swim but 10 percent faster requires a 33 percent increase in power. In the water, drag is everything. Active streamlining —avoiding water's drag—is the marine mammal's secret. And that, by shaping and positioning the body sleekly, rather than trying to pull powerfully, is the easiest way for humans to become more fishlike. In fact, kinesiologists estimate at least 70 percent of your swimming performance is determined by how well you streamline your body and only 30 percent by how fit or powerful you are.

So now we can begin to make that swimming-speed formula, $V = SL \times SR$, work for us instead of against us. First, you have to learn how to position your body so it moves as far as it possibly can with each stroke (SL); then you have to get fit enough to take those strokes at a higher rate (SR). But not too high.

Virtually every swimmer I see already has all the SR they'll ever need; it's the SL they're lacking. They always make their most dramatic improvements when they give up a bit of their SR in order to gain a lot of SL. So I always counsel swimmers to work on their SL first. Besides, energy consumption increases as a cube of muscle movement speed, so stroking twice as fast burns eight times as much energy. Not a great return on your investment.

I spent four years of college swimming trying to maximize SR and ignoring SL. No wonder I hit a speed ceiling. SL goes up when you use your brain. SR can only improve when you work on brawn, so its improvements are short-term and certainly can't go on forever. If you not only want to swim well but expect to do it for a lifetime, just look at the balance sheet. Then tell me which part of the swimming-speed equation you'd rather work on:

▶ SL is skill-oriented. You get better by improving your body's position or profile.

▶ SL improvements depend on brainpower. You use your knowledge, body awareness, and concentration to maintain sleek,

▶ SR is training-oriented. You have to work hard to build up your muscles and energy systems to make those limbs move fast.

▶ SR improvements depend on working your heart and lungs harder—*much harder*.

Swim Better Without Getting Any Stronger? Yes! — — — — — —

efficient positions in the water. That's nervous system—instead of aerobic system—training. The energy cost is minimal.

▶ SL can be improved at any age. There's no such thing as "too old," because it's skill-oriented, and our ability to learn or improve SL remains acute far into our 70s, allowing smart swimmers to gain speed well into middle age and beyond.

▶ SL improvements are permanent. Skills, once learned, become permanently imprinted in our "muscle memory." Invest time and effort in improving your SL and you won't lose it when you take a break from training.

▶ SR is age-limited. Eventually, your muscles just won't move any faster. The fuel for a high SR is provided by your aerobic capacity—the total amount of oxygen your muscles can burn to produce energy—which usually peaks at about age 40. That means your ability to increase your SR peaks too.

▶ SR improvements are temporary. They demand fitness and fitness is transient, as anyone who's had to quit working out for a couple of weeks can tell you. Stay away just a little too long and you're right back where you started, forced to do the work all over again to rebuild that capacity.

The best—and smartest—of the world's elite swimmers try to eke out further speed increases with the least effort by splitting the difference. If your stroke gets longer but the rate stays the same, you will swim faster. If your stroke rate goes up and you manage to keep the length the same, you will also swim faster. But if you increase both by just a little bit, you will swim *much* faster. They establish SL first, then try to gradually increase SR, giving up the least possible SL in return. It's a delicate tradeoff and one that the most successful swimmers practice unrelentingly.

Let's go back to that little speed statistic I mentioned earlier, the one about 70 percent of your ability to improve your stroke length coming from eliminating more of the water's drag on your body. It's not only true, it's the key to how great swimmers make their remarkable speeds look so graceful and effortless. That's no illusion. Relatively speaking, they *are* effortless. And learning to glide as far as possible after each stroke is the single most powerful skill they know. So we clearly want to devote the majority of our time and effort to becoming better "eliminators" when we swim.

It's a two-part strategy. First, play the game below the average speed line on your velocity curve (see illustration). Though you probably don't realize it, your body doesn't move at a constant swimming speed. During every stroke cycle you accelerate and decelerate, like a driver gently pressing and releasing the gas pedal. As you begin your stroke, the position of your arm and shoulder offers little leverage or power. Pull farther under your body toward your hips, and your arm moves into a much more effective position, one where the powerful torso muscles begin to help out. Up goes your speed. Then, as you finish the stroke and slice your hand out of the water, you begin to lose speed again. And you'll continue losing it until your other hand starts the next cycle.

Most people strain to swim faster by pulling or kicking harder or turning their arms over faster. They're trying to push the top of that speed curve a little higher before it slopes back down on the other side. Very wasteful. But if they worked on another part of the curve instead, they'd get where they're going faster and with much less exertion.

True swimming speed, of course, is not the top of the curve at all but the line that runs through the curve midway between the peaks and valleys—the average of your fastest and slowest progress during each stroke cycle. The amount of drag the water throws against your body is determined, in part, by how fast you're moving, and drag is much higher at the top of the velocity curve than at the bottom. So if you try to gain speed at the top of the curve, you bang up against a figurative brick wall. But there's far less resistance to speed improvement at the bottom, making it a smarter place to get faster.

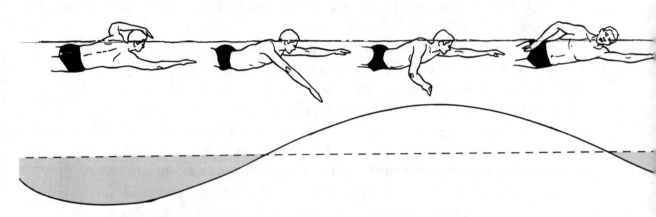

That's why *what you do between strokes is actually more important than how you take the stroke.* Look at the illustration. Where is your body moving slowest, which is just where you can most easily add speed? Right. During the recovery. So keep your body long, balanced, and sleek during the recovery, and you'll boost performance far faster than anything you can do at the moment with your hand.

It's welcome—and extremely unexpected—news to people who all their lives have been told that pulling and kicking harder and faster is the way to gain swimming speed. When I spring this fact on swimmers at my Total Immersion adult swim camps, they realize that what we'll be learning there, just as we'll learn in this book, is an assault on the conventional wisdom of swimming. It does nothing less than turn upside-down and inside-out the common understanding of what good swimming is all about. Great swimmers move so fast and take so few strokes not simply because they stroke powerfully but because their bodies keep slicing forward—quickly—for a long time after each one.

And it's an ability all of you can improve, whether you're headed

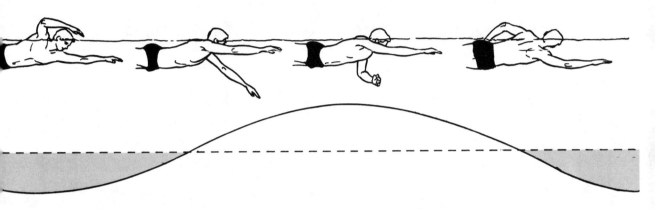

for the Olympics or just for the Y. You may have a perfectly fine stroke and still take too many, because your body lurches too abruptly to a halt after each one. You have no choice but to keep those arms turning over because you don't conserve the momentum you do create.

You need to learn a few tricks that will make you more slippery. They come naturally to fish, but the rest of us can pick them up too, once we know what they are. By the end of the next chapter, you will.

Chapter 3

The Slippery Swimmer

Resistance—it's just what you want in the weight room, but it gets in your way in other sports. If you've ever struggled to bicycle straight into a 30-mph headwind, you know why tapered helmets, Aerobars, even aerodynamic water bottles, were invented: to make you as compact and slippery as possible. The less surface area the air has to push on, the easier you move.

And in swimming you move through a medium that's 1,000 times denser than air! So while the need to become as streamlined as possible in swimming may be less evident because of the slower speeds you attain, it's actually more important. All efficient swimmers—which means nearly all the fast ones—seem to have a more instinctive sense of how to keep their bodies in the best position for slipping easily through the water, gliding as far as possible with the least possible effort.

I recently talked with Rick Sharp, Ph.D., the director of the International Center for Aquatic Research in Colorado Springs. He told me that his lab's research had recently turned up a surprising result, one that proved eye-opening to even some of the world's top swimming researchers. "We've discovered that the fastest swimmers generally produce less propulsive force than sub-elite swimmers," Sharp explained. "Obviously they're capable of producing more propulsive force, but they don't need it to go fast." In other words, they're faster not because of how powerfully they stroke but because of how *slippery* they make their bodies. For these elite swimmers, learning how to achieve this level of efficiency was a trial-and-error process, but the "secrets" of how anyone can do it have been around for . . . well, forever.

That surprises a lot of people who tell me they've finally come to one of my workshops because "I need to learn the new techniques. I started swimming back in the fifties and the strokes have all changed since then." So it comes as a nice surprise when I tell them that good swimming form is not like hemline lengths or tie widths—subject to today's fashion and tomorrow's obsolescence every time a new "discovery" comes along. There are principles of efficient swimming that can't go out of fashion because they're based on the permanent laws of physics, on how your body will always interact with the water.

What probably *seems* new to some people is that, remarkably, these principles have never really been explicitly taught until now, even though they were discovered long ago by naval architects who had to find ways to design the fastest and most easily driven ships of all time. These nautical scientists did all the work. Today, all we have to do is get into the pool and use what they found out, which, when applied to human rather than naval vessels, comes down to three cardinal rules for going faster:

1. Balance your body better in the water.
2. Make your body longer.
3. Swim on your side.

They sound like contortions. But they work like a charm.

Better Balance: The Biggest Energy Saver of All

Whenever a swimmer comes to me complaining that she needs to develop a stronger kick, I recall what I learned my first day on in-line skates not long ago. Like thousands of other people, I took up "blading" because it looked like a really fun way to get an outdoor aerobic workout. It turned out to be no fun at all, at least not the first time.

After maybe 15 minutes, I had to turn around and struggle home, confused. A dull ache in my lower back was bothering me so much I had to quit. "That's odd," I thought. "My legs are doing all the work."

I resolved to keep plugging away at this "tough" new workout, adding more distance to each session until I'd whipped those flabby back muscles—Rollerblading muscles, I presumed—into shape. But the next time I laced on my skates, I found out it wasn't weak muscles but poor form that caused my fatigue. Some skaters, I noticed, flowed along like syrup, their speed seeming to come from effortlessly swaying side to side. Others lurched along with choppy, labored thrusts. From a distance, I suddenly realized the difference was not back or leg muscle strength but weight shift. The good ones knew just when and how to transfer their weight from one foot to the other.

A smooth skater would lean all his weight on the left skate and then, *at just the right moment,* shift it all over to the right. Like all other lurching skaters, I hadn't caught on to this technique. My 200-pound bulk would teeter out way too far beyond my center of gravity, and those weary back muscles would have to snatch me back before I fell. Eventually, of course, they would have grown strong enough for the job, but by then I'd merely have turned into a strong, bad skater instead of simply a bad one. Smarter to learn balance.

Many frustrated swimmers make the same mistake. They know their hips and legs are dragging along far below the surface, and if they're lucky they also understand it's not only the most common stroke flaw but the most serious as well: It saps their energy faster than anything else can. So they grab a kickboard and grimly start churning out the endless laps they hope will strengthen their "problem" legs.

Only their legs aren't the problem.

The Slippery Swimmer — — — — — — — — — — —

That's because a poor kick isn't what's keeping them from swimming better. It's poor balance, just as I found that day on my blades. But in the pool it can be corrected practically on the spot. And when it is, these swimmers happily discover that a "weak kick" is no longer a problem. In fact, properly balanced, they hardly have to kick at all!

But proper balance in the water is not a gift of nature. It's something we earn through practice. The human body, you see, simply wasn't designed to float efficiently in the water. Evolutionarily speaking, we're put together to function well on land, where our long legs and low center of gravity are perfect for stability and mobility. Above the waist, we're mostly volume--the lungs, after all, are just big bellows. That means we're most buoyant between the armpits, rocklike lower down. It's only natural that our longer, heavier end wants to sink.

Churning your legs hard to compensate for the way nature put you together will wear you out. Worse, it's useless against the imbalance that's slowing you down. And it's the surest path to a poor triathlon, by the way, where the last thing you want coming out of the water— facing a bike ride and a run after that—is pooped leg muscles.

What you really need is a better way of getting those hips up where they belong.

And there is one. I call it "pressing your buoy." Here's how it works.

What happens if you push a beach ball into the water? Right. The water pushes it right back out. You have one place on your body that's buoyant like that—the space between your armpits. Call it your buoy.

Press your buoy into the water and the water will press back. But *keep* pressure on that buoy and you force the water to push your hips up instead. Just what you want. Simply letting water pressure ease them to the surface takes far less energy than trying to prop them up by churning away with your legs.

And you can help yourself by using the weight of your head like a counterweight. Remember, your body in water is like an unbalanced seesaw, its fulcrum somewhere between your waist and your breastbone. The longer, heavier end wants to sink. But use the weight at the opposite end and it levels off nicely. You do that by acting as though a steel rod ran from your waist through the top of your head. Keep that "connection" intact and you help your hips pop to the surface. Break the connection—lifting your head to breathe instead of turning it with your body roll, for example—and gravity will drag your hips and legs right back down again.

Later on, in Chapter 8, you're going to learn the simple pressing-your-buoy drill that makes all this automatic. You'll also start "swimming downhill," leaning on your chest as you go. With just a little practice, you'll discover that by pressing your buoy as you swim, you can make the water support more of your lower body's weight. Your suddenly lighter hips and legs will be effortlessly skimming the surface just where they belong. You'll actually feel as if you're swimming downhill.

The illustration below illustrates the difference between what your body looks like when it sinks unevenly, hips and legs dragging, and what happens when you balance evenly by pressing your buoy.

I don't promise it will come easily for everyone. The less buoyant among us (usually those uncommonly lean triathletes and runners)

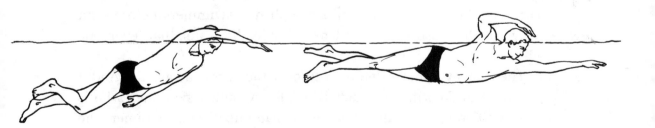

The Slippery Swimmer — — — — — — — — — — — —

find it a little tougher to get their hips all the way up. If you're among them, don't worry if your body rests an inch or two below the surface. You are not trying to float like a cork. You are trying to get your upper and lower body lined up nearly horizontal to the surface, with your hips and legs as close to it as possible. Do that and you'll cut drag enormously. Reduce drag, and watch what happens to your speed.

The most prominent benefit most swimmers will feel from learning balance isn't necessarily a stunning increase in speed. They'll be more likely to just feel more relaxed in the water. Once they realize that pressing the buoy causes the water to support more of their body weight, swimming becomes much less laborious. And a relaxed swimmer can do surprising things. One of my students, 52-year-old Don Walsh from New Jersey, became so adept at swimming relaxed that after completing the Swim Around Manhattan in nine hours, he related, "I felt good the whole way and was never tired during the entire swim."

Longer Boats Are Faster. Longer Bodies Are Too

When I was still pretty green at the coaching business, I was lucky enough to have two very gifted swimmers on my team, and smart enough to realize I could learn more from them than they could from me. The first thing I noticed was that no matter how fast they swam, they made it look relatively effortless. That didn't come as such a surprise—I'd observed this in accomplished swimmers before—but why did they also somehow look *taller* in the water than everyone else?

The best swimmers, I've noticed over the years, always do. And it has little to do with their actual height. A skilled swimmer who is only 5'10" looks taller in the water than an unpolished swimmer who is 6'2", and it's no illusion. Better swimmers do "swim taller"—something anyone can learn—and because they do, they go faster. It's one of the fundamental principles naval architects have been using for over a century to design fast ships.

In the 1830s, a fever broke out among clipper ship owners to shatter the record for the fastest ocean crossings. The boats had only sails for power and couldn't simply install bigger engines, so more speed had to come from better hull design. W. Froude, a naval architect in England, tested various vessel shapes in a tank to learn which would produce the fastest design. His key discovery was that, all other things being equal, a vessel's drag decreases as its length at the waterline increases. Translation: longer boats go faster—and easier. To this day, his calculations, known as Froude numbers, are used to predict the potential speed of various vessel designs.

What applies to clipper ships applies to you. In the vernacular of naval architecture, your body—along with racing yachts, rowing shells, or canoes—is a "surface-penetrating moving body" subject to many of the same laws. If a longer vessel can go faster, a taller swimmer can too. And taller swimmers do. In the 100-meter freestyle, swimming's premier sprint event, the fastest men in the world average about 6'6".

There are ways you can swim tall too, regardless of your height. And they are important to learn because they put mathematics powerfully in your favor. Take a hypothetical six-footer who swims the mile in 25 minutes. Feed him some growth hormone so he sprouts up to nine feet. He doesn't train any longer or harder, he doesn't get any stronger or fitter, he doesn't change his stroke in any way. He just gets taller. But his improved Froude number predicts that he can probably do the mile in 18 minutes!

Fine. But what if you're "only" 6'0" and at 30-something quite likely

The Slippery Swimmer — — — — — — — — — — —

to stay there? Well, as far as the water is concerned you can still grow, stretching your six feet to nearly nine feet from fingertips to toes by simply extending your arm overhead. And if you can stay in that extended—taller—position for more of each stroke cycle, you improve your own Froude number enough to go much faster on the same amount of energy.

Here's a simple experiment to prove it. Under water, push off the pool wall as hard as you can with your arms at your sides (the six-foot position) and glide as far as possible until you surface. Then do it again with your arms straight and streamlined overhead (the nine-foot position). See how much farther you go?

That's also the secret for swimming taller, what my mentor, Bill Boomer, calls front-quadrant swimming, or FQS. In the illustration below, consider the waterline as the x-axis and an imaginary vertical line through the shoulder as the y-axis. The two lines divide the swimming space into quadrants, the front quadrant being the one in front of the shoulder and under the water.

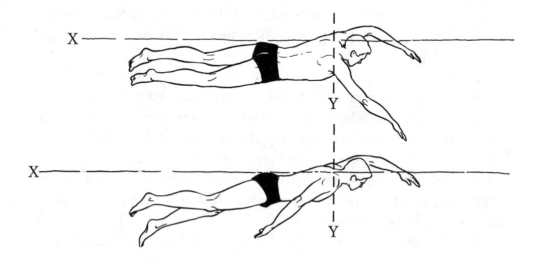

FQS swimming means always keeping one or the other of your hands in that front quadrant. (At the beginning of each stroke, of course, both hands are there.) It's really just another way of saying "swimming tall," of lengthening your bodyline and making you taller than you really are. Leave your right hand out in front while the left is stroking, then begin stroking the right just as the left returns to the front quadrant, and so on. One hand doesn't start until the other one's nearly back. Leaving each in place just a split-second extra can make a big difference in your Froude number.

Common sense? Well, actually not so common. Why else would almost all the swimmers in my weekend workshops show up the first day as rear-quadrant swimmers? Why else would I have worked so hard when I was in college at being a rear-quadrant swimmer? Because it's easy to fall into the trap: "I move my body by pulling my hands back, right? To get it going faster, then, I just move my hands back faster, right? Gliding along with hands stretched in front? All that will do is slow me down!"

So my college swim strategy was like a bathtub windup toy: Dig in and pull back as soon as my hands touched the water. Unfortunately, it guaranteed that I would spend precious little time with either hand out in front of my head. I swam short, and it showed. I took 24 to 25 strokes per length, compared to the 14 or 15 I now use in my mid-40s. Stroking fast was making it harder to *swim* fast.

Some people, as I was, are rear-quadrant swimmers by intent. But others can't help it—as soon as their hands enter the front quadrant, they're driven down and back. Their arms are "heavy" because of the weight they're supporting, weight that would be distributed elsewhere if their balance were better. Face it: You just can't be an FQS swimmer unless you're also a well-balanced swimmer. But whether or not your rear-quadrant tendencies are intentional, FQS is something no one does naturally. You have to know it matters, then consciously work on making it a habit, confident that you're taking another important step to becoming a faster and more efficient swimmer.

Done right, FQS is nothing less than a revolutionary way of thinking about what your hands do for you when you swim. Suddenly, you understand they contribute far more to your speed when used as bodyline extenders than when used to push water back. Once you've discovered that, you can use them more effectively to make you taller in a couple of ways.

First, use your hand to lengthen your bodyline before using it to stroke. This should be a true reaching action, like stretching up to a high shelf for something just out of your grasp. It should be as easy as extending your hand all the way forward first—not down—when it goes into the water. But for some people, it's not that easy. As soon as their hand hits the water, years of bad habits take hold and the arm automatically heads right for the bottom. It does, that is, until I ask them to pretend they're reaching for the wall as they would on the last stroke of each lap. As far as the muscles are concerned, that's different—now the arm goes out nice and straight and long. And the body glides along more easily behind.

Don't rush the process. Leave your hand extended before starting to pull back. Don't be in a hurry to start stroking. Chant silently, if it helps: "Enter, e-x-t-e-n-d, pause, and pull." Just let your hand keep gliding forward out there, reaching as long as possible before you begin stroking.

Second, make your arms better bodyline extenders by taking a load off them—literally—so they feel weightless. If you're pressing your buoy as I told you to, and if you're keeping your head's weight supported by the water and in line with your torso, you're already there. But if you are there, you're in the happy minority of the already balanced. If not, you'll want to work on a weightless arm using the specific drills in Chapter 8, before trying to actually swim with one.

When you do, you'll find that the weight of those heavy arms and hands usually comes from one of two places:

1. You haven't put all your weight on your buoy, so some of it has gone back to your hips and legs, and they're sinking. To compensate, you're driving your hand and arm quickly down and out of the front quadrant. You're becoming shorter.

2. You're lifting your head—even the littlest bit—as you breathe. That shifts more weight to your hand, which has to support it. Down it goes too fast, over and over again, every time you breathe.

I promise it will take you a fraction of the time to learn that it took me. Swimming is not only my livelihood but my love, and I've been working on my stroke efficiency for years. But I was looking for speed in all the wrong places, minutely examining every movement of the hand through every centimeter of the stroke, and feeling lucky to shave maybe one stroke from my average every two years. Then I hit on the weightless arm and lopped two strokes off in just a matter of weeks. Then another after that. Believe me, when a professional coach's count per 25 yards tumbles from 16 to 13 strokes after almost 30 years of trying, he practically wants to tattoo instructions for the technique onto anyone who'll stand still. I'm *that* convinced.

So is coach Jacki Hirsty. Hirsty, a Masters swimming world-record-holder in the women's 35–39 age group, had been coaching with me on and off for five years. But it wasn't until we taught a Total Immersion workshop together in Boston that she heard about the weightless arm, a technique I'd finally polished up enough to share with students. The day after the workshop she tried it herself. She cruised through a set of 400-yard repeats faster than she had in several years, and on top of that, her stroke count was actually lower.

The Slippery Swimmer — — — — — — — — — — — — —

Don't Swim Flat; Swim on Your Side

There's still another lesson swimmers can learn from boat designers: how to make their bodies fly like racing yachts instead of plowing along like scows. What are the fastest sailboats you can think of? Maybe the America's Cup contenders? With only the wind for power, they go like, well . . . like the wind. What's the slowest *powered* boat you can think of? It has to be the cargo barge. Load it up with as much horsepower as you want and it will still crawl. Well, we all have the choice of swimming like barges or America's Cup yachts.

One of the most enduring myths about our sport is that the correct position for swimming freestyle is lying on your stomach, turning your head to the side when you need a breath. Red Cross-trained instructors have taught millions to swim that way. And the few the Red Cross missed automatically swim that way too, because they just feel more comfortable and secure flat on their stomachs.

But it's wrong. You don't swim freestyle on your stomach if you want to be any good (and by the way, you don't swim backstroke on your back either). The fastest, most efficient swimmers in the world cut the water on their sides, rolling from one side to the other with each stroke and staying on each side for as much of each stroke cycle as they can. The advantage is simple to understand: You slip through the water more easily that way than on your stomach.

Let's go back to naval jargon for a moment. You'll recall that your body—along with yachts and barges—is a "surface-penetrating moving body," and all of those are subject to the same physical laws because they all slice the surface as they go. (Submarines, torpedoes, and fish—as well as butterfly and breaststroke swimmers—hang out below the surface and are subject to slightly different hydrodynamics.) One of those laws is that drag or resistance goes up by the *square* of the distance the water travels to get out of your way. Twice as far equals four times as hard. So would you rather swim like a barge, pushing water in front of you, or like a yacht with the fluid slipping easily around you? Dumb question.

And you've actually understood this principle since you were a little kid, holding your arm out the window of the car. When you held it straight up, palm flat against the airflow like the traffic policeman's stop signal, the wind pushed it hard. Then, you bent your elbow so the palm faced down, fingertips pointing forward. Wow. Hardly any pressure.

Same thing applies to your (surface-penetrating) body in water. As you swim, water goes mostly around you to get out of the way. Very little slips underneath. On your stomach, you're like a barge with its "broad shoulders" forcing the water to move so far that it's constantly pushing along a huge volume of water in front. Yachts, on the other hand, even if they're broad in the beam, are knifelike up front, so it's easy for the water to go around, as shown in the illustration below.

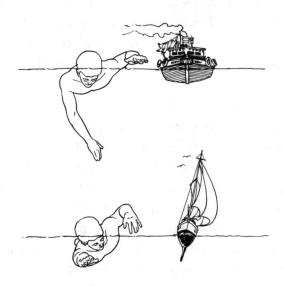

The Slippery Swimmer — — — — — — — — — — — —

When you swim like a yacht, cutting water on your side, drag may be half as much as when you swim like a barge.

I know. You can't stay on your side forever. But you can go from one to the other as you stroke. The world's fastest swimmers roll until they're nearly perpendicular to the water and glide there for as long as possible in each stroke cycle. You should try to do the same.

Rolling also helps make your body a little longer. Prove it to yourself this way: Stand facing the wall closely, one arm straight overhead, palm flat against the surface. Leave your hand where it is, and turn your body to the side, then back again several times. Notice how your hand slides up as you turn, and down as you turn back, making you "taller" each time you turn sideways and "shorter" as you turn back to face the wall? Same thing when you roll to your side: You swim taller.

Given all these advantages, you obviously want to roll on every stroke, ending up as close to a side-lying position as possible at the end of each one. The smartest thing you can do then is stay right where you are—on your side—as you return your arm to where it will reenter the water. As a consequence, you glide in the fast-moving side-lying position the whole time you're not stroking. And you glide farther and faster because you're not pushing all that water in front of you.

Done this way, freestyle becomes graceful, powerful, a feat of intelligent body engineering instead of a tiring exercise in plowing through the water. It becomes a series of long glides linked by quick rolls as you stroke and change sides. Each time, your body has a working side—the one you're pulling with—and a sliding side—the one that's making your body longer so the pull delivers all the speed and distance it can. The longer you stay on your side in each stroke cycle, the farther and faster your body will travel. Swimming also becomes much more restful and a lot less work. It even looks easier.

And that may drive some people crazy. While traveling to one of my workshops not long ago I was a guest at a Masters group's workout. After a single set, one of the swimmers in my lane came over to me and, with just a bit of an edge in his voice, said, "I can't figure out how you're keeping up with us. You don't look like you're *doing* anything." Well, compared to everyone else, I wasn't. They were churning their arms steadily, splashing mightily, and "getting the work done." I was like a sailboat, quietly gliding and resting on my side between strokes—and staying right up with them. Without roll and glide, they had no choice but nonstop arm turnover if they didn't want to stop dead in the water between strokes. Of course my swimming didn't look like a lot of work. Compared to theirs, it wasn't. It may even have looked like cheating.

So why doesn't everyone swim this way? Are they gluttons for punishment? No. But even if most swim instructors didn't actually *discourage* people from something as valuable as rolling—which they do—you'd still see more "flat" swimming than anything else because that's how we feel more comfortable. Rolling to the side makes us feel unsteady, tippy, out of control. So we barely tip to one side or the other, and we certainly don't stay there a nanosecond longer than we have to. Face-down just seems right.

It's that old bogeyman, bad balance, and if learning to do it flat on your stomach took some practice, wait until you have to balance on your side. It's not natural, it's not instinctive, and it's difficult to learn without concentrated, conscious effort. But until you have it, you're going to avoid rolling and you'll settle for being a barge. And you don't have to settle, not when the skill drills in Chapter 8 give you a step-by-step approach to ultimately feeling as slick as a racing yacht.

When I first said that streamlining your body probably accounts for about 70 percent of your potential swimming improvement, I expected those raised eyebrows. I always get them in my swim clinics too—until we jump into the pool and start shedding resistance-causing bad habits left and right. "I've never seen the bottom slide by so fast," someone will say, or someone else will report that they've just cut six strokes from their normal count for 25 yards. The drills we use are the same ones you'll find in Chapter 8 of this book. Your results should be just as exciting.

But even I have to admit one thing: You can't glide if something didn't push you along in the first place. That's called propulsion, and just because I think it's overrated doesn't mean it can't be dramatically improved. First, though, you must forget the idea you probably have of needing powerful shoulders to drag the rest of your body down the pool. Then I'll tell you what *really* does the job, and how you can make it happen more powerfully.

Chapter 4

Tuning the Engine:
Finding—and Using—Your Swimming Power

"If your body were a motorboat, your engine would be in your hips. Your hands are actually nothing more than the tips of the propeller blades."

I learned that from my mentor Bill Boomer, and at first it sounded backward to me too. After all, I'd directed countless swimmers to spend hours in the weight room building powerful arms and shoulders. And now a coaching maverick was trying to tell me I'd had it all wrong? That they're not what moved me through the water in the first place? That I'd essentially been misleading my swimmers?

Well, yes, that's almost *exactly* what he was saying. When I paused to think about it, I realized that what he was saying made perfect sense even though, at the time, virtually no one else saw it that way. "Swimming is the rhythmic application of power" was another Boomer aphorism, an innocent but actually quite seditious statement since it meant that rhythm (which swimmers seldom worked on), not power (which they worked on all the time), is what's actually at the heart of creating propulsion in brilliant swimming. Good body rhythms give you the power that the arms and shoulders simply deliver. And rhythm movements *must* originate in the body's center or core, not at the extremities (the arms and legs)—just the opposite of how swimmers have always tried to do it.

Boomer had seen to the heart of swimming propulsion, understanding the underlying physics of swimming while the rest of us were still just slapping the water. Propulsion—how we produce the force that actually moves us through the water—did not work the way we all thought it worked, Boomer told us. But few were open-minded enough to listen at the time.

You may be wondering, freshly convinced from the previous chapter on streamlining, whether your shape and balance might be all that really matters. But stop and think: Even though 70 percent of your potential speed improvements will indeed come from learning to slip through the water more easily using the techniques in Chapter 3, that still leaves another 30 percent you can tap. And that 30 percent comes from learning a more economical and effective style of creating propulsion.

It's the second half of what I call the eliminate/create process: First eliminate drag, then create more power. That's exactly how you should work on it too. Start by understanding what it feels like to be in harmonious balance in the water, then shape your body so it evades frontal water pressure well, then learn to apply rhythmically powerful movement. We're now about to start installing the engine on your seaworthy vessel.

Not only does this put first things first, it saves the easier work for last. For while reducing drag is certainly not complicated, improving propulsion is simpler yet. If you've ever despaired of mastering all the seeming rocket science of "S-strokes," hand shape and pitch or vortex patterns recounted in other swim books, we're about to make it much simpler and more lucid.

Better yet, the whole propulsion process follows from the techniques you've already learned to reduce drag. You're still swimming "inside-out," first generating power by rolling your body from side to side, and only then using your hands to deliver that power to the water. Once you master "eliminating," you're already doing most of what you need to do for "creating." So it's not a new course, just the second semester of the one you've already grown familiar with.

Get Hip to Your Swimming Power

I'll start off by telling you something that, at first glance, may make little sense: Your arms are not that important. Well, not the way you may think. Power in most sports—swimming included—originates much lower down in your body. In most cases, the arms are just the "delivery system."

Picture the smooth arc of a John Daly drive off the tee. Or the explosive serve of a Pete Sampras. Or the powerful *crack!* as Ken Griffey, Jr., drives yet another one out of the park. Then think of the power it takes to drive a ball over 300 yards, or blast one over the net at 130 mph, or send it arcing 450 feet or more into the stands. What arms, eh?

Well . . . no. Arm swing may be what is most visible to us, but it's not what's doing the work. Arm swing is actually the last—and least powerful—of a linked series of actions, each of which takes its momentum from the one before. As the pitcher releases the ball, the batter's first action is to cock his arms and shoulders away from the ball (a so-called plyometric contraction like winding up a spring, storing energy that will later be released in the opposite direction). Then it all begins to unwind. He starts by stepping toward the pitcher as his hips take up the rotation and in turn power the torso around, which drives the shoulders toward the pitch. The shoulders pull the upper arms through, adding speed. The upper arms pull the forearms, and only after the forearms have gotten up to speed do the wrists snap, completing a crack-the-whip chain that finally drives the ball. Huge forces are generated by a combination of powerful muscles—mostly in the butt and torso—moving a maximum amount of mass with perfect timing.

So why do the same people who would go to their hips for their power if they were standing at home plate or on the tee think they

Tuning the Engine: Finding—and Using—Your Swimming Power — —

ought to swim by spinning their arms like a windmill? A powerful stroke, like the one that results in a home run, should be driven by rhythmic rotation of the body starting, as does the batter's, at the hips. Remember the last technique we covered in Chapter 3, the drag-diminishing body roll? Well, the same roll that lets water slip around you also conveniently produces virtually all of your stroking power. Yes, it's all in the hips, and you've already begun to direct them into purposeful rotation. When you do this, you're using the body's most powerful muscles, the gluteals (the butt muscles), to move your center of mass from side to side. And powerful muscles moving a large mass generate impressive force.

The arm and shoulder muscles don't really amount to much by comparison, so why struggle to use them as your engine? You wouldn't try to move your car with your windshield-wiper motor, would you? Those arm and shoulder muscles are, however, superb stabilizers, and the way to take advantage of that is to use them to hold onto the water.

If nothing else, muscles that hold on don't get hurt like muscles that are trying to act like workhorses. Think of your arms and shoulders as the engine, and invariably you'll push them too hard. The best you can hope for is wearing yourself out too soon, and you will. Your arms quickly lose their punch because they're doing way too much, while the true workhorse muscles lower down are loafing along. Worse, you could be heading for an injury. Mother Nature really wanted your shoulder muscles to simply hold together and stabilize the joint, setting your arm in a maximum-leverage position where it can better hold the water against the powerful forces developed by your body roll. She never envisioned them driving your arms through the water by the hour, like a Mississippi River sternwheeler. So make this joint do most of the work moving you down the pool, and sooner or later Mother Nature is going to send you a big error message.

Tap the power in your real power source, however, and watch what happens. Where did all this fitness, this feeling you could go on forever, this freedom from fatigue, suddenly come from? Even the previously exhausting little trick of trying to accelerate your hand during the second half of each stroke—something all swimmers have heard of and at least have to try—seems easy now.

How come? Because swimming with just your arms makes as much sense as trying to swing a bat with just your arms instead of winding up the rest of your body first and *then* unleashing all that momentum. Do the latter and you'd be lucky to manage a feeble infield grounder. Home runs come from the hips. So do swim trophies. And the energy that powers the process in swimming comes from a simple trick of coordinating that whip-cracking energy chain as it unfolds. Let me explain.

A little formula from your high school physics class, $F = M \times A$, probably went right out the window after your final exam. Well, it's time to get it back. When you do, you'll have a new source of swimming power that won't cost you any energy.

"Force equals mass multiplied by acceleration" is what the equation tells us, and back then even those dozing in the back of the room knew that if either value on the right side of the equals sign went up, the resultant force would go up too. So in this case there are two ways to increase the force. One is by keeping mass the same and increasing acceleration—in other words, don't put more of your body into it, just move your arms faster. If you want to waste energy that's the very way to do it, since energy expenditure balloons as a *cube* of any increase in muscle speed. To move your arms twice as fast takes eight (2^3) times more work.

But what if you turn this around? What if your stroke power could somehow go way up and the effort stay pretty much the same? Couldn't you swim much faster without getting tired? You could and you can. It's done by increasing the "M" in the formula. Simply move more of your body mass all at once when you stroke. Your arms go at the same speed (perhaps you can even slow them a bit), but now your entire torso is powering them. Feel that new force. Make your hips the first part of the body to move in each stroke, and watch your power grow.

In other words, let your hips set your stroke rhythm, since they're the core of the movement when you're doing it right. Try to set it with your arms instead and they'll quickly go off on their own, breaking the chain and essentially disconnecting themselves from their engine. If you were a car, your transmission would be gone. Lead with your hips instead, and your stroke will be both rhythmic and powerful. Your arms will be happy to follow.

They're Not Hands Anymore: They're Anchors

"Well and good," I hear the mutters, "the hands aren't important. They don't pull us along through the water the way we've been taught since grade school. But they must do *something*. What?" Don't worry. I'm not advocating hands-free swimming. But since they account for perhaps as little as 10 percent of your overall efficiency, I've left the hands for last. As I've said over and over, swimming isn't complicated. Swimming *instruction* is complicated. And that's partly because it's usually delivered by the dumptruck load, all at once and with no priorities. Try to concentrate too early on what your hands are doing, for example, and you'll divert concentration from the far more important body movements. Once your streamlining and balance and rhythmic power are well underway, however, you're entitled to wonder how to best use those appendages out on the ends of your arms.

The best thing you can do is leave them there—not only on your arms but in the water. Several times earlier, I challenged the outmoded notion that you pull water back with your hands. You don't. Now's the time to reply to the obvious question: Then what *do* you do with them? And my answer is, *make them stand still.* Anchor your hands in the water, which is precisely what all great natural freestylers do.

Alexander Popov, the world's most dominant freestyler, does even better than that. On every stroke, he takes his hand out *ahead* of where it entered. After he slices his hand in, he grabs and holds the water, using his "grip" to slide his body past his hand, almost as if he had grabbed a rung on a submerged ladder. Making the hand stand still in the water is one of the key "creating" skills of world-class swimmers, many of whom appear to be born with it. But it's nothing the rest of us can't learn.

I'm sure by now you're not surprised to hear that this too starts with hip roll. But now things get more interesting. Power is power only when it has something to act against, and the hips couldn't roll with nearly as much force if your hand didn't first stabilize your upper body at the beginning of each rotation. So the combination of stretching your arm forward at the beginning of the stroke and leaving it there actually does more than "make your boat longer." First, it keeps you from wasting energy in the puny stroke you'd be able to manage with only weak shoulder muscles to pull and no other power or leverage to speak of. Second, it lets you "load the spring," storing up the energy that you'll release in the stroke to come. Remember that batter cocking his arms and shoulders, coiling away from the pitcher before leading into his swing with a hip turn? The golfer's and tennis player's backswing is the same kind of energy bank, storing muscle tension in the torso which will later be released in the swing, like pulling a bowstring taut before shooting the arrow.

Same thing in your stroke. Your hand enters the water and reaches forward just beneath the surface—and I mean *reaches,* like stretching for something barely beyond your fingertips on a high shelf. Next, with your hand as far out as it can possibly go and your body rolling onto its side, your arm anchors itself into position. Now, with the torso moving and the arm fixed, your upper body becomes increasingly taut, just like the golfer's backswing. And just like the golfer, you're storing up that energy for the action to come—the drive off the tee, the roll of the hips.

Alexander Popov knows just what it feels like. And if you'll walk over to the wall for a minute, you can too. Face the wall and reach up with, say, your right hand, sliding it as far up as you can. Now rotate and lift your elbow slightly off the surface. You'll feel a stretch in the muscles surrounding your armpit. Turn your left hip and shoulder about 45 degrees away from the wall and you'll feel tension building in the powerful latissimus muscle (in your back, below the armpit)— not on the weak shoulder muscles. That's Popov beginning his stroke.

And that's why you grab the water and hold on, just as you resisted the air on your hand out the car window. With practice, you can keep that sense of pressure constant and steady throughout the whole pull.

So there you have it. Jerk your hand back immediately after plunging it in and you've started an exercise in futility as it slips water from one end of the stroke to the other. Bald tires on an icy road. Instead, slip your hand in, anchor it to get ready for the pull, and keep your grip as you move your arm down and back using robust body-roll muscles, not weak shoulder muscles. Welcome to the world of studded snow tires, a V-8, and four-wheel drive to boot.

But still, watch your traction. Tune in to how fast your hands are moving as they pull. Compare the speed of your hands pulling back with the speed of your body moving forward. If they're going faster, you're slipping, not gripping. Your hands should never move faster than your body. Keep practicing until they don't.

Some

By now

expec

one

after

wron

sional

this:

cally

your

ment

Thi

conve

worki

your l

to ign

more

—fati

these

do all

then,

makir

crucia

worki

ance,

yours

windo

One final heresy. Your hand gets from here to there just fine by following a straight line. So if any of the white-coated swimming theoreticians come after you with their clipboards and pointers, sputtering about "S-strokes" and "insweeps" and "outsweeps" and "pitches," tell them you don't sweep and you're not a pitcher. Tell them you simply pull your hand in a straight line back under your body (right down the center of the body, of course) and through the hips. If it was good enough for Johnny Weismuller, it's good enough for the rest of us. Don't even bother about slicing your hand back outside the hips as you finish. Just press straight through. If your hips are moving as they're supposed to, they'll just roll to the side, conveniently out of the way.

But remember: First a sleek boat, then a powerful engine, and only after that a good propeller. Don't spend more than 10 percent or so of your available training time fussing with perfect use of the hands. They're a footnote at the end of the line, and you want to start at the beginning where the most important action is. And conveniently, that's how the drills are organized for you. First things first.

So let's have a look.

at first. Your challenge is to change that, to make them second nature. This means that if you want to go beyond just understanding how to swim with maximum efficiency, if you want to make it the way you swim *all the time,* an absolute habit, you have to *practice* specific stroke modifications. And practice, and practice. Think of it as a new kind of training, training that targets the nervous system instead of the aerobic system.

Don't worry. This isn't a thinly disguised "consolation prize" alternative for people without the youth, or the power, or the genetics, or the hour-upon-hour of time, to do "real" workouts. It is, in fact, the way the true champions, who understand their sport, train themselves. And Alexander Popov is the best example I can think of, the fastest and *most efficient* swimmer in the world today.

For nearly five years, from 1988 to 1992, the American swimmer Matt Biondi had a hammerlock on that title. He deserved it. Biondi swam more efficiently than any of his rivals and was undefeated in his specialty events. During the 1992 Olympics, with Biondi having already announced it would be his last meet, Popov seemed the heir apparent. For several years his coach had videotaped and studied Biondi, using the champion's stroke—the world's most efficient—as a model for his rising star. Coach and swimmer worked tirelessly to master Biondi-like movements.

The showdown came in Barcelona, in the final of the 50-meter free. That event is the ultimate efficiency laboratory, the purest sprint event of them all—one length, no turns, over in maybe 20 seconds. Popov and Biondi stood on the blocks in adjacent lanes in the middle of the eight-man final heat, the gun went off, and the field streaked down the pool. Popov touched first in 21.8 seconds, Biondi right behind at 22.0 seconds. A new Olympic champion had been crowned. But what most amazed analysts was that Popov had not only beaten Biondi by a comfortable margin, he had beaten him thoroughly at Biondi's longest suit—stroke efficiency. Popov had taken 34 strokes, Biondi 37. The time gap may have been just 1 percent, but the three-stroke difference, an *efficiency gap* of nearly 10 percent between the world's two best sprinters, was nearly inconceivable.

It was just the beginning of a new efficiency standard. In the years since, Popov has continued to dominate the sprint events, raising the bar again and again for efficiency and speed. No swimmer on the horizon threatens his stranglehold on the sprint because Popov can swim at startling speeds with much less effort. While everyone else is working furiously, the supremely efficient Popov just seems to be gliding majestically along.

The lesson this champion can teach the rest of us is that it might not have happened at all. Had he simply swum as others did, obsessed with moving briskly up and down the pool for several hours a day—working out—he would have developed less-efficient stroke habits and turned into just another swimmer in the pack—albeit a very good pack. Instead he was trained to practice precise technique so it became utter habit. On race day, as his oxygen debt mounts, heart rate soars, and muscles throb, along with his opponents', everyone else's form breaks down—if only a little bit; his doesn't, and even that modest edge is enough to win every time. His sterling performances are proof of the victory of practice over training, of having a nervous system that's at least as well trained as your aerobic system—working smart rather than working out.

Learning Versus Training: How We Build a Skill

The Total Immersion learning system has outperformed all other methods of teaching adults to swim because it's the only one that teaches new skills the way we learn them best—in small pieces. As far as your body is concerned, the job of pumping up an arm muscle is altogether different from teaching that arm muscle to move in an efficient swimming stroke. Skills involve feelings, habits, movements that feel awkward at first and must be made to feel natural. So learning a skill is best organized into a step-by-step process that breaks the big job down into bite-size parts, then recombines them so gradually that each step is easy to master. And the most effective way to tell if you've got it all right is by feel. Every movement you'll be asked to practice in this program is designed to give even the newest swimmer a taste of what the key parts of the swimming stroke *feel* like to an elite athlete. Up to now, every swimming expert has told you how the strokes of an Olympic swimmer *look*. But looks are hard to mimic. Feelings are much easier.

However, just doing the same thing over and over won't make you an expert at anything either—including the freestyle swim stroke. We've all heard of the hapless gentleman wandering aimlessly down New York City's 57th Street carrying a violin case, finally stopping a passerby to ask, "Excuse me, but how do I get to Carnegie Hall?"

The sardonic reply: "Practice! Practice! Practice!"

Snappy but only half-true. Suppose he *did* practice, but without hearing. What if he just scraped his bow over the strings each day no matter what squawks came out, happy that he was getting his arm muscles in shape so he could spend even more time scraping out ugly sounds the next day?

Ridiculous? Don't answer until you're absolutely sure that's not how you—and probably most of the people you know—have been practicing your own swimming for years. Musicians dedicate monumental amounts of rehearsal to produce beautiful sounds, but the quality of their practice time matters to them far more than the quantity. So it should be for swimmers. Practice, we must come to understand, merely makes permanent whatever you happen to be practicing. Good *or* bad.

If you're like most swimmers, making deposits in your aerobic bank account is your main concern. And of course you know that you do that by keeping your heart working in the aerobic range, usually for an hour or so. In essence, a swim workout creates extra heartbeats. If your aerobic training range is 120 beats per minute and your walking-around heart rate is 80, an hourlong workout will create 2,400 extra heartbeats. A perfectly good return on your investment in a nontechnical sport like running. But not in swimming.

In the water, you're ringing up a far more important tally during the course of those 2,400 heartbeats, and that tally is the 2,000 or so strokes you take. Each one leaves a faint impression on your central nervous system, forming a pattern of movement—a *habit.* If you've been swimming for a few years, those stroke habits have become pretty strong. Now stop and think: Since the 2,400 "fitness" heartbeats impact only about 30 percent of your swimming performance while the 2,000 "skill" strokes affect about 70 percent, as we said earlier, which one deserves more of your attention? Right. You're beginning to think like a Total Immersion swimmer already, and you're getting ready to see swimming as a matter of muscle memory, not muscle power.

Muscle memory is what coaches call familiar, habitual patterns of movement. Thanks to muscle memory, you can ride a bike, tie your shoelaces, and type on a word processor without stopping and thinking about it. Once you learn a skill well, you can just let your muscles take over. Unfortunately, they'll take over just as aggressively if you've learned a skill badly. And if you think they're interested in giving up those habits, think again.

Muscle memory is like an old LP that has been played hundreds of times. The stylus, tracking in the record's grooves over and over, gradually wears them deeper. In sports, your muscles and nervous system become more and more "grooved" to automatically execute a movement the same way. Fine if your stroke is efficient. Not fine if it's not. Practiced for long enough, a bad stroke becomes almost immune to change.

Almost immune. But it can be done. What it takes to break old, inefficient habits so new, efficient ones can take their place is the determination to first erase, then replace. You have to make sure that every one of those 2,000 strokes in your workout hour is as much as possible like the economical strokes of skilled swimmers. Settle for less and you're training to become a less accomplished swimmer.

So why do most lap-and-fitness swimmers—and even medal-hungry competitive athletes with coaches—spend most of their pool time working out, trying to improve their physiology with *more* laps or *harder* laps or less rest between repeats? They're on a downhill road. Faltering concentration, fatigue, trying to keep pace with the clock or keep up with another swimmer, will all gradually erode their efficiency. They end up practicing their mistakes.

Start your change today. Begin your transformation from a strictly workout swimmer to a practice swimmer. As a workout-only swimmer, strokes were just something that got you from one end of the pool to the other. Laps *were* the point. The tally was sacred. As a practice swimmer you'll realize that each stroke is an investment in your swimming future, each lap a chance to either build your stroke into a well-oiled machine for carrying you fast and far or to break it down into a laborious mess. A practice swimmer works no harder, instead squeezing more good out of the same—or even less—effort.

And while all this is going on, a curious thing will happen to your muscle strength, just as it happened to Alexander Popov's. Even though strength is no longer your holy grail, it will grow, but it will be the muscles that move you most efficiently growing stronger. Popov got to be the best in the world by *practicing*. And while he was doing that, his muscles grew fit enough to break world records. To get the most from your physiology, be less concerned with how many yards you swim and more concerned with how many yards your body travels each time you take a stroke. You'll still get the extra 2,400 heartbeats and your muscles will still get a workout. What can you lose?

Make Those 2,400 Heartbeats Work for You

During my weekend workshops, after patiently explaining for hours that swimming is 70 percent mechanical efficiency and only 30 percent fitness, that practice is more valuable than workout, and urging participants to regard fitness as "something that happens to you while you're practicing good technique," I still expect curiosity over just how fit a swimmer needs to be. Someone always asks: "Yeah, but how many yards a week do I need to be ready for a 1,500-meter triathlon swim leg?"

Fitness *is* important, I tell them, very important, but not for the reasons you've probably thought. The reason you want to be in the best possible shape is not to be a powerful athlete but a precision one—so you can keep using your high-level technique over longer distances, at higher speeds and higher heart rates. That's the reason our program starts in the easiest possible way: with efficient movements, over short distances, at low speeds, and at low heart rates. You gradually build your capacity to *hold that form* longer, harder, and faster. Sounds a lot like race preparation, doesn't it?

So the big role of fitness is to help you hold your form. But all fitness is not alike. I compete in Masters swimming on a semiregular basis. When I do, I usually target a regional or national championship in the spring, devoting about five months to intense, focused preparation. After the meet I cut back on my swimming and start running several times a week for a change of pace. And every time I do, no matter how hard I've worked and how well-conditioned I've gotten myself in the water, my muscles rudely remind me that as a runner, I'm a rookie.

It's the same thing that happens right in the pool when you switch strokes. If I've done mostly freestyle training, I'll be lucky to feel good for the first half of a breaststroke race. The second half crumbles into a desperate struggle against muscle fibers that are quitting one after the other because they simply haven't been trained. Breaststroke muscles are different from freestyle muscles. If they're new to the job, they won't do it for very long.

Now let's cut the distinction finer still. You even use different muscles for swimming freestyle with good form than you do with poor form. Train sloppily and your better-conditioned poor-form muscles will be in great shape. You can guess what happens next. Come race time—or even a longer-than-usual workout—your well-intentioned brain will give your body the right pep talk ("Okay, now, let's really hold good form here!"), but if you haven't trained the muscles it's talking to, their answer will quickly be, "Forget it." You'll be stuck with "sloppy-swimming" power.

Nobody can get away with that whether they go for speed or distance. Neither top speed nor effective endurance can be achieved with pinch-hitting stand-in muscles. If you swim the 100-yard freestyle in a Masters meet in 60 seconds and would like to do it in 58, your primary goal is to train yourself to stay efficient as you move everything faster. You'll get those two seconds and more. Or say you do the much longer 500 yards in nine minutes and would like to do it in eight. Now the strategy is to stay efficient longer. If you used to get a shaky stroke at around 200 yards and can now hold form right through the last 300, you're going to make a serious dent in that finishing time. None of that happens unless, like Popov, you program your muscles to do it.

And more than your muscles are working to form every stroke. What do you think fires them in the first place? Right. The nervous system. And though this part of the training process is almost always overlooked, the nervous system also stores away everything you do during that hour or so you're in the pool. Lap after lap it selectively recruits muscle "motor units" to move your arms and legs in certain ways, learning as it goes. Just as with the muscles themselves, you're either training it to be habitually efficient or habitually inefficient. Routinely let your efficiency slip over the course of an hour and that's just what your nervous system will be ready to do for you next time and the time after that. It will remember. You need to make sure it remembers what you want it to.

Learning Skills With Success Drills

New triathletes are often amazed that they can pick up a bike after a cycling layoff of 20 years and feel like they never missed a day. No rustiness, no relearning—*zoom!* Off they go. That's because the ability has been there all those years; it's just been in storage. The skill comes out again easily because it's fairly simple—cyclical, rhythmic, hands and feet fixed in place. You don't have to repolish much besides your balance and steering, and that doesn't take long because all the time we spent doing it as kids left a powerful and permanent imprint on our nervous systems. The neural groove on your bike-riding LP is already deep. The needle never jumps. And it's a much simpler tune to play.

Swimming, of course, is nothing like that. Neither is tennis. And though on the surface there seems little to unite those sports, they have far more in common than most athletes—and most of their coaches—realize. In fact, the way to understand how the body best learns a skill and why the Total Immersion training system is so effective at speeding that process along is to watch someone with a good coach learning his or her way around the tennis courts.

First, the basics. Tennis and swimming are both motor-skill sports that also take strength and endurance for success. In swimming, skill and stamina combine to move you up and down the pool faster, farther, and easier. In tennis, skill puts the ball right where you want it, while stamina chases down the return and holds stroke-crippling fatigue at bay.

So you'd think swimmers and tennis players would learn useful training techniques from each other, but they don't. You'd think they'd realize their practices are a lot alike—or should be. But they don't. Swimmers try to improve just by swimming more. But they don't.

Tennis players wise up faster. Many start the same way by "just doing it," digging up a tolerant partner and smacking the ball back and forth. They usually don't get very far that way. In the beginning especially, they spend more time chasing down wayward balls than hitting rallies. It soon dawns that they won't improve much if they can't even keep the ball in play.

So they sign up for lessons with a tennis pro. "Pro," after all, has a nice, crisp ring that sounds so . . . well, so professional. "Coach," as in swimming coach, implies someone who just tells you how to sweat. Too often, both implications are on target, to the great advantage of the tennis player.

The tennis pro understands that the most important thing to do for his or her students is teach them, not train them. They need to master skills that will make them competitive on the court, and the pro needs to help those students learn faster and with the least possible confusion. That means starting off with the simplest possible movements— small segments of the basic strokes. In the forehand lesson, for example, the student simply stands with his feet planted in one spot, racquet held back, while the teacher lobs the ball so that it bounces up softly at waist height and practically into the strings of the racquet all by itself. A successful return is guaranteed.

Even so, the first 10 or 20 are awkward, mechanical, erratic. Gradually they grow smoother, more accurate, more consistent. The learning and sorting-out have begun as muscles and nerves catalogue and memorize the difference between swings that work and swings that don't. If a ball flies out of bounds, the student "erases" that swing from muscle memory. If it ends up just where she wants it, she replays that one over and over. Not only can she see her successes and failures, she can feel them. The jolting *thwwoong* of a vibrating mis-hit rockets right up her forearm, while the precise "pong" of the racket's "sweet spot" feels and sounds solid and true. Each time, the experience is "written to disk" in the nervous system where, eventually, hundreds and thousands of such "experiments" in movement skill begin to build a vast neuromuscular database of experiences. Only one or two of those resulted in hitting a good ball, of course, so gradually the student's muscles figure out how to do just those. That's when the pro sees something especially rewarding: The returns are now virtually automatic. Step one is complete. The basic forehand has become encoded in muscle memory.

Learning any new motor skill is a similar problem-solving, trial-and-error exercise. But too much error can be so discouraging that enthusiasm goes right down the drain, and with it the chance to improve. The secret is to practice something you can do, not something you can't.

An easily mastered basic skill becomes the springboard for a more advanced one, and so on. You see results every step of the way.

That's why the pro waits until step two to hit the ball around, making it seem a little more like a real game of tennis. "This should be fun," the student thinks, until her nice, new, smooth, and coordinated basic stroke turns to shreds again as she now tries to second-guess where the ball is going to be before she can figure out how to meet it with her racquet. Think for a minute what's behind just getting to the ball. Mind and muscles watch the ball's trajectory and direction, compute where it's going to land, rush to that spot, and get the feet and torso into position to swing before the ball arrives. Only then do they get to use that now-familiar basic skill—returning the ball. Moreover, they now need a unique program for each shot depending on where the ball lands and how fast it's going. It may take dozens of such lessons just to develop a rudimentary tennis game. Obviously, the only way to make sense out of the wilderness of skill-building is by a stepwise system of learning, and practice that's organized to take the student through it.

Which is exactly what's been missing from most swimming instruction. Swimming coaches spend so much time training and so little time teaching that few have ever really thought about how to break down their equally complex sport into a series of fundamentals that can be taught step by step. Instead, their stroke advice comes in scattershot bursts, not in a series of "success lessons" that can be mastered quickly and that automatically lay the groundwork for the next skill. Their swimmers spend too much time swimming the whole stroke, never quite able to achieve fluency in all its parts. With Total Immersion, we teach like the tennis pro instead.

With one important difference. Tennis players have a big advantage over swimmers: They can see their results, and they can see them right away. Ball goes right or ball goes wrong. Swimmers have nothing that obvious to guide them. Unless someone is standing poolside bellowing at you like a coach as you swim, you have to rely on how things feel inside your water capsule. So your skill-building drills must be designed with "feeling feedback," letting your nerve endings be your coach.

Let's go back to the most critical improvement you can make—getting your body balanced and stable. It doesn't come naturally, it doesn't feel natural, and new swimmers who balance by instinct are as rare as a balanced federal budget. It takes most people years of trial-and-error practice to figure balance out on their own, if they ever do. Our skill drills skip trial-and-error entirely and, by telling you what feeling you should aim for, put you through each critical step of the process quickly. You can learn balance, for instance, in 30 minutes or less. Drill by drill, cutting out hour after hour of dead-end experimentation, we put the whole learning process into high gear.

So that's swimming, the Total Immersion way. Realizing now that your skills carry you a lot farther than your fitness, you don't work out anymore—you practice. And you repeat to yourself as often as necessary: *"Fitness is something that happens to me while I'm practicing good technique."* And practicing, and practicing, because now you also know that old habits die hard, especially old muscle habits. If you've been swimming without instruction for several years, in fact, you've probably had so much practice at inefficient swimming that your body is an absolute champion at it. To learn a better way of swimming, you have to unlearn the one you're stuck with, which means never doing it again. Every length you swim with poor form makes it harder to improve.

And the way we'll make sure you've swum your last length with poor form is to use the same step-by-step strategy that tennis pros perfected long ago. There's no reason for racquet sports to be any better than water sports at helping athletes build good technique. Tennis players may have gotten wise sooner, but with Total Immersion, swimmers are now there too.

The tennis program works so well because it meters out a series of easily mastered mini-skills that gradually link together into a smoother, more powerful game. Efficient swimming can now be taught in the same logical, step-by-step process. It all starts with the best friend your swimmer's nervous system ever had: the skill drill. It makes the complex simple, the intimidating comfortable, and the difficult easy. In the next chapter, the mini-skill finally arrives at the pool.

Goodbye, "coach." Welcome to your first lesson with the "swimming pro."

Chapter 6

Skill Drills: The Fastest Way to a Faster Stroke

Sometimes I think that if we left it up to the experts, the only people who'd dare to get into a swimsuit would be elite athletes with burning Olympic aspirations, and children too carefree to have any aspirations at all. Because the "experts" all warn us: An efficient swimming stroke is a prize with a staggering price. So many motions to coordinate! So many ways to go wrong! No wonder it takes countless hours of practice to reach a decent level of skill and smoothness. Why, the grooming of an Olympic-level swimmer usually begins not long after kindergarten—at the age of seven or eight! And even then, for maybe five years, the basic skills are hammered in over and over before the first hints of training for strength and endurance.

Rubbish. For an Olympic aspirant, maybe that's what it takes. But it doesn't have to be that way for the rest of us. And for adults, who generally haven't had that kind of time since they were kids themselves, it simply *can't* be that way. So without professionals to guide them and with few hours to invest, grownup swimming hopefuls usually just plod through the laps, hoping that as the mileage piles up their strokes will improve. Instead, as we said in the last chapter, they're making things worse by practicing their mistakes. And the more they swim this way, the harder it will become to snap out of it someday. They may finally reach a state that one of my campers wistfully called "terminal mediocrity."

It used to be that your only hope for breaking out of those bad habits was to find a good coach. Not anymore. There are ways you can turn things around and begin learning improved skills all by yourself, methods we'll teach you in the next few chapters.

It all starts with what I call the stroke saver, otherwise known as the skill drill. Think of the skill drill as your personal and powerful Batman against the Joker of bad swimming habits, able to root them out thoroughly, replacing them with sound, new ones almost automatically. The skill drill is—no exaggeration—the quickest and most effective path to masterful swimming. Skill drills are the core of the successful method I've used for over two decades to help swimmers of all ages to improve dramatically. One of the reasons is that the drills are so easy to learn that even inexperienced swimmers can become their own best coaches.

I don't care if you've been frustrated for years. You can dramatically improve your swimming in just hours with these technique drills, a process that has no way of happening when you plod mindlessly up and down the pool practicing your mistakes.

With conventional instruction, the learning process can consume tedious and frustrating months. Drills work by speeding up your learning curve, and that's no small feat. Even excellent swimmers who look like they must have been born with their effortless grace have probably invested months, or more likely years, in polishing that smooth, almost balletlike way of moving. Sometimes a coach's guidance did the trick; in other cases their exceptional intuitions were enough. But either way, the process is the same: Over time, they've hit on breakthrough moments when their stroke feels just right, moments that the body immediately seizes and—just like the body of our tennis pupil—stores in a catalogue of similar "how-to-move" experiences. Eventually, the catalogue becomes comprehensive enough to produce an extremely smooth and highly efficient way of swimming.

It's a process that never really ends—which is one of the most exciting things about swimming. There's virtually no improvement ceiling when it comes to good technique. Whether you're a beginner just "getting your stroke wet" or an expert looking to medal at a national meet, there's always something left to work on. The refinements just become increasingly subtle. After winning an astounding seven Olympic medals in 1988, Matt Biondi admitted, "I still see every practice as a learning experience because I've come to realize that even now, I only understand about ten percent of what efficient swimming is all about."

But trial-and-error is a very time-consuming way to pick up an involved skill like swimming—as any self-taught tennis player can tell you. So the Total Immersion method takes this haphazard and painfully slow process and organizes it for you. The result is a step-by-step system of drills selected so any swimmer can recreate, in an organized, convenient, and reliable way, his or her own "flashes of learning" to put into the catalogue. Suddenly, you can capture those elusive feelings of being "in synch" whenever you want instead of stumbling onto them now and again by accident. Best of all, you can practice them again and again.

Still, as all the king's horses, all the king's men, and Humpty-Dumpty all found out, parts are just parts until you put them back together again. When you go back to swimming the whole stroke after polishing pieces of it in your drills, your body reassembles them naturally into a much-improved whole. Your nerve endings have done your learning for you by taking "snapshots" of sensations that elite swimmers feel consistently as they knife through the water, and assembling them into a complete photo album: your stroke.

Now, if you suspect that we're really just drawing out the learning process with all this pulling apart and putting back together, I'll let you in on the four powerful physical facts that make skill drills such a potent stroke-improvement tool:

1. **Fact: Your Muscles Need a Dose of Amnesia.** Muscles have memories, as we said. Habits are powerful. And that's just what the stroke you've been using for years has become—a habit. Probably not a good one either. And because you've been struggling for so long, your muscles have become very good at moving like that. They'd prefer to keep right on doing it, in fact.

Stroke drills are powerful enough to break that cycle because they're disguised. They're so different from your normal motion that your muscle doesn't recognize the movement and insist you do it in the same old way. You practice new skills on a neuromuscular blank slate without having to erase anything first.

2. **Fact: Small Pieces Are Easier to Swallow.** Learning specialists tell us we pick up skills faster by breaking a complex movement series into manageable segments for practice. Because the swimming stroke is made up of so many finely coordinated parts, it's virtually impossible to digest the whole thing. So our Total Immersion stroke drills are "bite-size," reducing the whole stroke into a series of mini-skills, each of which can be quickly mastered. Then you simply reassemble these building blocks into a new, more efficient stroke. Each drill teaches a key skill, and we present them in the order the body best understands. It's like putting up a building: The first drill is the foundation, each succeeding drill adds a floor, and mastery of each step gives you the key to solving the next one.

3. **Fact: Instead of Trial and Error, It's Trial and Success.** Drills stack the learning deck completely in your favor. You can't lose. Because mini-skills can be mastered quickly and easily, you begin practicing

smooth movements right away. The more you practice each smooth movement, the more it becomes your new habit and crowds out the sloppy old one. And the less time you spend swimming with your sloppy old one, the faster you learn to swim better. That string of successes boosts your motivation and self-confidence—and studies have shown that happens faster when you believe in what you're doing.

4. Fact: It's Language the Body Understands. Telling a muscle what to do is a little like teaching French to your poodle: You get rapt attention but not much retention. Conventional stroke instruction suffers from the same weakness. It's too rational. It tries to get to your muscles through your mind, even though muscles really don't respond all that well to being lectured. Think about it. First you have to hear, or possibly read, a description of what you're going to attempt. Next, you try to figure out what the movement will feel like. Then you instruct your muscles to imitate that feeling. Finally, you ask yourself if you got it right. If you didn't, you try it again a little differently.

Drills bypass all those vague translations. They simplify—and accelerate—the learning process. From the very beginning, you teach your body how it should *feel* when you swim well.

The great part is, skill drills are self-adjusting. The more you need them, the better they'll work for you. When beginners practice them they learn basic skills in big chunks and rough edges get smoothed off quickly. Experienced swimmers, doing the same drills, tune in naturally to far-more-subtle refinements, bringing a higher degree of polish to skills they already have.

And the more you have to learn, the more you should drill—up to four times as much as your normal swimming if you really have your work cut out for you. It may be the only way to make headway against

Skill Drills: The Fastest Way to a Faster Stroke — — — — — —

bad habits so hardened through the years that they're all but concrete. Think of it this way: every lap of drilling, which you can learn to do well quickly, is positive reinforcement for your swimming. Every lap of swimming may pull you back toward old habits. I tell my workshop pupils to ask themselves: "How much swimming can I *suffer,* as I try to teach my body new skills?"

And though every swimmer is different, drills work for most with incredible speed. *Everyone* I've taught them to has improved. I can't think of any other swim instruction method that can claim that. And they'll work even faster if you:

1. **Think *Before* You Swim.** Every drill is a problem-solving exercise, and nothing beats the old-fashioned virtues of patience and persistence when you're trying to solve a problem. With each new drill— and every time you do refresher drilling the first month or two following this program—take these steps: *First, a few repetitions* just to remind your muscles of the problem the drill is meant to solve, such as moving your head and torso together as you roll your body to breathe. *Next, several repetitions* to work out the solution. *Finally, several more repetitions* spent "memorizing" that solution so it comes naturally. Now you "own" it.

2. **Do It With Feeling.** These drills get your muscles talking to your brain instead of the other way around. If your brain is listening, it's going to learn what the motion or skill you're practicing feels like when it's done right. And when it learns that, it can start to replay it automatically. Feels right, *is* right; and the mind-muscle connection begins to work more smoothly. So the first few times you work on any new drill, *stick with it for at least 10 to 15 minutes* to firmly imprint the new sense into your memory so the brain can eventually go by sensa-

tion rather than by thought. Don't be rigid. Experiment with subtle adjustments. See how much control you really have, and what happens when you alter these new movements even slightly. Eventually you want your body to take over from your mind, automatically doing what at first required all your concentration.

3. Don't Drill Yourself Into a Hole. Marathon drill sets can easily do more harm than good, a case of too much of a good thing. If you're tired and can't concentrate, you won't drill well, and drills build good skills only when they're done well. *Practice them in 25-yard repeats, resting 10 to 15 seconds between.* Every rep should feel a little smoother and more relaxed, a little more precise and economical. If not, reread the instructions or go back to the previous drill and polish that one up before returning to the one that's giving you trouble.

4. Take Your Drills Out for a Test Swim. Work no more than 10 to 15 minutes at a time on a new drill. Then, *alternate drill lengths with swim lengths,* trying to make each swim length a little more efficient—taking fewer strokes—and a little easier. Compare your drill and your stroke. What felt better in the drill? Good. Try to get more of that feeling into your stroke. When you're pressing your buoy, for example, your hips and legs will suddenly feel light as they skim the surface instead of dragging along behind you. Focus on that. See how much of it you can feel when you're swimming. Think of it as your chance to do a virtual-reality lap with a Popov stroke. And keep at it. Lasting improvement won't happen instantaneously.

5. If the Fin Fits.... Here's a paradox. Drills are designed to get your body so well balanced that you won't need much of a kick to swim well. A weak kick won't slow you down anymore. But you will need a bit of propulsion from your legs to drill well. Your body's moving slower—and lower in the water as a result—while drilling than when you swim. A bit of kick helps compensate. If yours is weak, you'll waste so much energy struggling for the right body position that you won't have much left to drill with. Slip on a pair of fins, and you'll be able to pay attention to what matters—the fine points in each drill. By the way, for skill work bladed fins are far better than the cut-off, so-called "speed" fins, particularly if your ankles don't flex easily yet.

Drill-and-Swim: Some Assembly Required

In my program, skill drills are little short of magic—absolutely the best way to improve. But they can only do that if you fit them properly into the puzzle of the whole swimming stroke. And just as particular puzzle pieces have to fit into the whole in a particular way, drills don't go just anywhere in your swimming workouts. Drill without a plan and you could miss the whole point.

Drills, you see, can be the potato chips of swim training: so addictive you begin to lose your appetite for other things. Things like swimming. I've seen people become absolutely terrific drillers and do little-to-nothing for their swimming stroke in the process. They've let good drilling become an end in itself.

That's not necessarily bad if all you want is to be fit. Drills can be a workout all by themselves, sometimes more of a workout than swimming would have been. In fact, you could easily stay in great shape doing nothing but drills without ever taking a single conventional stroke. But wouldn't that be a little like carefully assembling all the parts to a classic MG and then never building the car? Yes, drills can be fun, and they do offer scenic byways to the monotony of the turnpike—swimming the black line back and forth and back and forth—but let's not get carried away.

Drills build skills, but they build them best if you integrate and alternate them with swimming in an organized way. Remember, drills are 1. the simplest way to teach your muscles new movement patterns, and 2. the best way to turn up the volume on feelings that tell you when you're swimming well. Alternating with swimming will give your drills the most powerful influence over your stroke. They'll give you a *sensory target,* a feeling you're looking for. And when you have a feeling you're looking for, you can better focus your practice.

Your progress in this program will be steady and reliable because we've organized those sensory exercises into logical sequences, just the way your body wants to learn them. Each sense-skill builds on the one before it. You can't lengthen your stroke, for example, until you've first gotten yourself balanced.

Be patient. Drill-swim will work. It can't fail, in fact, because it employs natural learning methods. Your body is a brilliantly intuitive instrument, with a faultless sense of what it needs—given enough information. As you drill and swim, you'll sense what works best and you'll gradually capture that and make it your own. But remember: This learning instrument works best when allowed to learn at its own pace. You didn't pick up all your bad habits overnight and you're not going to pick up new ones overnight either. Just one repetition of a new drill may start the learning process, may even begin tracing a faint neurological imprint that will make the next repetition easier and more natural. But real skill requires that the groove be cut deeply through many repetitions, each done the same way.

So don't try to force-feed yourself. Patient, persistent repetition of the drills to get the feeling right, alternating with swim laps where you take that feeling and put it right into your stroke, is the best way to let drills work their magic. Use short repeats and short sets. Fresh muscles train well. Fatigue—mental or physical—brings sloppiness. And sloppiness is what you'll be practicing once you're tired or bored.

Just 25 yards of a drill, followed by 25 yards of swimming, followed by a short rest, will give you the highest-quality practice. Give it all you've got for maybe 10 minutes or so. Then give your brain a rest by doing something that requires less concentration—a few laps of stroke counting, for example, to see how much more efficient you've become.

And as judges are fond of reminding lawyers, you need to keep to the point. Don't work on one thing in your drill and drift off into thinking about something else during the swimming you do right afterward. Focus, focus, focus, in drills *and* in swimming. If you worked on pressing your buoy while drilling, don't start thinking about hip roll on your swim length. You'll never finish anything.

And I'll go even further. Your drill guidelines in this book's swim lessons suggest five or six points to concentrate on in each drill. That's about four or five too many to do all at the same time. You can think about exactly one, and one only, with enough clarity and focus to do it well. Get greedy, go for two or three at the same time, and they'll all get fuzzy. You won't do any of them well as your concentration leapfrogs all around. Instead, force yourself to do a little drill triage, with my permission. Decide which points you clearly feel make the greatest difference in your stroke and spend more drill lengths thinking about those. Keep the exact same point in mind on your next swim length. (See the appendix for sample practices that do this.) Focus, focus, focus.

And gradually, when you're ready, wean, wean, wean. Stretch farther and farther the distance you can swim with better form before heading back to the drills for a reminder. For that *is* how it will happen, maybe three steps (or strokes) forward, one step back. In the beginning, you see, that neurological tracery is still faint. It may take you three or four drill lengths to even get a clear sense of what it is you're practicing, and it may be all you can do just to hold that sensation for one full swim length once you get it. So your ratio of drill lengths to swim lengths could easily be as high as three or four to one. As you continue practicing, though, your body will get it faster and faster. Eventually, one drill length might groove that feeling back into muscle memory firmly enough to shift right over to a swim length.

Little by little, you'll work up to two lengths before your form begins to wobble and need a drill refresher. Then three lengths. Then. . . . But be patient at stretching the distance. Eventually, you'll be able to take the new, improved you for much longer cruises. Feels good, doesn't it? Well, congratulations. Your old habits are on the run, your muscles are now beginning to remember the right stuff, and the stroke that was holding you back is losing its grip on you. Now it's time to pry loose a few more of its fingers. Hang on to your concentration but take off the training wheels. Let's start some full-stroke swimming.

If "sensory skill practice" sounds to you like an ad on late-night cable TV for an adult videotape, I need a minute of your time before we go any further.

Because SSP, as I call it, is actually something a good deal more important—well, more important to an improvement-minded swimmer, certainly. It's nothing less than the capstone, the finishing touch, on the whole Total Immersion learning process. Each Total Immersion drill focuses on some aspect of swimming described in chapters 2 through 4. Each drill, in turn, heightens the kinesthetic or sensory experience of how "right swimming" *feels*. In SSP, we practice swimming while focused on that feeling.

In sensory skill practice you take all the ingredients of an efficient stroke, the ones you so meticulously developed in your skill drills and rehearsed in your drill-

swim sessions, and make them permanent. Automatic. Yours. Good form that your body follows instinctively, free at last of those nagging reminder lectures from your brain. That daunting mental punch list—Am I pressing my buoy enough? Is my body long? What about hip roll? Did I reach for the far end?—is edited down to a simple and smooth body check: Does it *feel* right?

Teach your senses what "right-swimming" *feels* like, you see, and they'll take over and do more to help you hold good swimming form than a video camera ever could. Automatically and accurately.

The challenge is figuring out how to take full advantage of your new movements. At this point they're like individual sheets of music that you can play well in whatever order they turn up on the music stand. But if they're ever going to become a concerto, they must follow a certain coherent sequence.

So what we do in sensory skill practice is to arrange your skills in a logical order and "play" them that way, since some let you unlock others, like opening a series of nested Russian dolls. For though I preach consistently throughout this book that the way to become a better swimmer is to cut swim time and drill, drill, drill, there comes a point when you have to swim, swim, swim. But what a difference now! You've gotten over your black-line fever. The odometer no longer rules your life. It's not how long or how far but how well. You finally know what it feels like when you've got it right. Your job now is to make sure it always feels that way from now on.

Don't be surprised if your body at first has trouble trusting this "swim by feel" approach. After all, it's just the opposite of what many of us were told to do by our school coaches. Back then, we worked on *ignoring* instead of paying attention. Face it: The way most of us were schooled, if you took athletics seriously you didn't shrink from getting falling-down tired. And a good coach, in those days, was someone who could help your mind wander off to something other than how miserable you were feeling, to "disassociate" from the workout so you'd forget how exhausted you were and manage to keep on going just a little longer and a little longer after that. Like my peers—and probably like yours—when I paid any attention at all to what my body was doing, it began and ended with wondering how well I was using my hands to paddle.

So that was the extent of my technical focus when I came back to regular swim training in my late 30s. And today, it very probably is still yours.

When it gradually became clear that body positioning is so much more important to effective swimming than endurance or strength, I knew I would have to completely reverse my idea of training. Instead of *telling* my body what to do, I would start *listening* to it as it reported in from thousands upon thousands of nerve endings and informed the brain—as it had always tried to do—what was working well and what wasn't. Now, though, instead of ignoring all this information, I would guide it into the smoothest possible technique and focus the lion's share of that attention on my torso—the body's power source—instead of my arms and legs.

My first sensory experiment was with pressing the buoy. As a coach I'd been teaching it to butterfliers for nearly 20 years. Leaning on the chest in that stroke made it conspicuously easier for them to bring their hips up. But it wasn't until around 1990 that it occurred to me that the same principle of lifting the hips and legs to reduce drag might work in freestyle too. As a test, I asked a couple of new swimmers, who were struggling especially hard, to give it a try. The difference was immediate, and so dramatic you didn't need to be a professional coach to be impressed with the results. I realized that it could help my own swimming as well. And probably everyone else's.

But the habits of coaches, even young ones, die just as hard as anyone's. True, those first tentative shifts into greater torso-awareness sparked an immediate improvement. But I'd already been swimming for 25 years, and long habit kept my mind drifting back to what those hands of mine were doing. The moment I lost concentration, I knew I had also lost body position. The sudden drag on my back half told me so. Obviously, if I wanted to hold on to this improvement, or any other improvement for that matter, I had to figure out a way of making it automatic and instinctive. "In the bank," so to speak. Then I could go on to the next.

So I did what any good athlete would do: worked as hard as I could at nailing that improvement down. What I nailed down instead was the realization that long swims or hard swims simply break down the critical ability to concentrate. They actually give new life to old habits. The only thing that worked was short repeats where I ignored the clock, other swimmers, my hands, and what I might be having for dinner. Just one thing was allowed on the mental table: chest pressure for keeping the hips light. Total sensory absorption. And it worked.

Best of all, it continued to work for every piece of the skill puzzle I wanted to add. In the next two years I packed more efficiency into my stroke than I'd managed to eke out in the previous 25 years. You can do the same.

If It Feels Good, Do It. And Do It Some More.

The difference between sensory skill practice and drill-and-swim is the difference between cycling without training wheels and cycling with them. Drill-and-swim is training-wheel swimming: If you start to go wrong and lose your balance or form, you can fall back on the drills for support. Sensory skill practice takes the wheels off for as long as you can leave them off. It challenges you to pedal straight and true, as far as you can go, before starting to wobble again.

Here's how it works. On each drill length, you zeroed in on one specific sensation—light hips and legs, longer body, weightless arm, rolling hips—then held onto it as you swam, like practicing a bar of music over and over. The more lengths you swam that way, the deeper that feeling sank into your neurological memory bank. Eventually, the feeling sank in deeply enough to become your natural stroke.

Or did it? Your objective in sensory skill practice is to find out. Take the same catalogue of desirable sensations and see how far or how fast you really can swim with one or another of them. Consciously practice skillful swimming—and nothing else. Instead of counting laps or racing the clock or another swimmer, you're focused on using each lap and every stroke to imprint specific skills more and more deeply, more and more permanently.

In a sense, sensory skill practice puts the finishing touches on the learning process. In step one, you learned new ways of moving using drills. In step two, you integrated those movements into your swim stroke. Now you're testing your ability to swim consistently better—with consistently less thought. It's the drill work without the drills. Drills teach you what these sensations feel like; then you take them into your stroke and simply practice *feeling like that* as you swim.

But this is far more than just "mop-up" work. Many of these movements, remember, are alien to our nervous systems at first, so almost any workout will eventually break down your new and still-fragile form. Frankly, it will take all your patience and determination to make the new form natural and instinctive. But it will be worth it.

The best news is that you can count on the fingers of one hand all the drag-minimizing SSP movements you need to practice, as you'll see in the following list of five. The "how-to" part sounds a lot like the drills, and it is. But now, you're not drilling anymore. "This ain't no practice run," as the saying goes. This is taking the more efficient you and really *swimming* with it:

1. Swimming Downhill: This tests how well you're able to press your buoy to improve your balance, bring your butt to the surface, and reduce drag. Learn to do it right, and improvement is instantaneous. Guaranteed.

Hold On to This SSP Feeling: Just as you did on the pressing-your-buoy drill, tell yourself you've got to lean on your chest as you swim. You may feel as if you're swimming downhill. That's good. Other swimmers have said it's like someone pressing down on their shoulder blades as they swim. And a runner recognized the feeling from her sport: She felt as though she were leaning forward slightly to balance and brace her body against a punchy headwind. When you get it right, your hips will feel lighter, your kick far easier. In fact, relax your legs completely so they can simply follow along. Keep leaning and skimming the water. If you do it consciously and religiously, you'll eventually do it instinctively.

2. Swimming With a Weightless Arm: The key to front-quadrant swimming, which makes your body taller and faster in the water.

Hold On to This SSP Feeling: When you swim downhill, putting all your weight on your buoy, your extended arm should feel virtually weightless as it practically floats out in front of you after it enters the water. Your fingertips thrust effortlessly toward the far end of the pool until you *choose* to apply pressure to your hand and begin the stroke. You also feel elongated—your weightless arm makes you taller each time you stroke, and even taller as you roll to breathe.

3. Reaching for the Far Wall: This complements the weightless arm. Some swimmers can't fight the impulse to dive right into the stroke as soon as their hand touches the water. Not good. It makes them shorter, makes them slower, and makes them unbalanced. This breaks that habit.

Hold On to This SSP Feeling: If your hands stubbornly jerk down and back as soon as they enter the water, try this. Pretend every stroke is the last of your lap, the one where you reach out for the pool wall. Swim every stroke of the lap that way. *Reach* for the wall. As you're reaching, feel your shoulder press alongside your jawline. (If it's a breathing stroke, you should feel your ear pressing into the shoulder of the extending arm.) Then, when you can't reach any farther, begin to pull. One more point: reach *slowly* for the wall; your hand shouldn't be extending any faster than your body is moving forward.

4. Hand-Swapping: You've learned to extend your arm and lengthen your body, but how long should that "extender" stay out there before the other hand shows up? Hand-swapping tells you when to begin stroking the extended hand as the recovery hand comes around.

Hold On to This SSP Feeling: Does it seem like you're waiting to start your stroke just a little longer than you're used to? That's it! The whole point, in fact, is to put off pulling with the extended hand until the other one is just about to reenter the water and take its place in front of your head. As we said, this keeps your body longer—and faster—for more of each stroke cycle. But you won't be able to do it unless your extended arm is weightless, so go back and master that one first if you haven't yet.

You may have to do a little drill to get hand-swapping right. "Whoa. Back to drills again?" you protest. "Why are you making me repeat a grade in this swimming school of yours?" Don't worry. This is the hardest to learn of all the sensory skill targets because it involves subtle stroke-timing adjustments, but it's worth mastering by any means necessary. And a modification of the catchup stroke (see drills in the appendix) is the best way there is of mastering it—with a couple of changes.

First, breathe normally (not every other stroke as you do on that drill). And don't pause with one hand covering the other in the extended position. Start the new stroke as soon as your recovery hand touches the top of your extended hand. Practice this until it feels comfortable, not clumsy.

As soon as it does, start the following sequence:

1. a length of full catchup
2. a length of three-quarters catchup (stroke starts just before the recovering hand touches the extended one)
3. a length of half-catchup (stroke starts when the recovering hand reaches the elbow of the extended arm)
4. a length of quarter-catchup (stroke starts as the recovering hand passes your forehead)

When you get to this point, you've got it.

Initially, hand-swapping feels exaggerated and unnatural. This four-step practice guides your body into gradually feeling at home with the movement. Cycle over and over through this sequence and you'll soon pinpoint just the right moment to swap hands.

5. Moving Your Midsection: If swimming on your side still feels awkward and your hips resist your brain's message to roll, practice this one.

Hold On to This SSP Feeling: **Nothing ambiguous about what to do here. On every stroke, just point your belly button toward the pool side wall on each side. Not literally, of course—you'd need a ball-bearing-mounted spine to roll that far. But with that target, you will move better. And as increased roll begins to feel more natural, you can relax because you'll be doing it without thinking. Just make sure you're always shifting your midsection rhythmically from side to side. Now you're swimming with your powerful hips, not your puny hands. When you want to swim more powerfully yet, put more *snap* into your hip rhythm. When you want to swim faster, put more *speed* into your hip rhythm. Keep it up until your whole sense of stroke rhythm is the rhythm of your midsection moving back and forth, not that of your arms churning.**

Sensory Skill Practice: Easy Does It

1. Start by alternating SSP with drill lengths that broadcast the same message. The similarities between the two will give you a clearer and stronger grasp of the exact sensation you're after.

2. Limit your practice to 25-yard (or single-length) repeats at first. Swim the first half-length without breathing—not to see if you can do without air but because your body will absorb the new sensation faster if it doesn't also have to attend to the mechanics of breathing. Then segue smoothly into normal breathing, but stay strongly and narrowly focused on the sensation.

3. Go slowly. Your body is more sensitive to new sensations when moving gently through the water. You'll have plenty of chance to pile on speed later.

4. At the end of each length, stop and think a moment about what you just did. If you were swimming downhill, did your hips feel lighter and your kick easier? If you were reaching for the wall, did you feel your body lengthen? If not, go back to the related drill, which will accentuate and clarify the feeling you're trying to create.

5. Do enough lengths for the sensation to settle in. You'll know when that happens, but I'd look for it at around eight to ten repeats while you're working on something new.

continued

And when you've got all that under your belt, keep your momentum going by:

1. Gradually lengthening your repeats to 50, 100, perhaps even 200 yards. It's not too ambitious to want to eventually swim a mile or more with your new efficiency intact, if that's the length of a race you plan to swim.

2. Blending two sensations in one length (e.g., swim downhill with a weightless arm, or reach for the wall with a weightless arm, or swim downhill moving your midsection from side to side).

3. Alternating sensory targets on each length (e.g., on a series of 50s: swim downhill on the first 25, weightless arm on the second 25).

4. Pumping the throttle: swim a series of 50s 25 slow/25 faster. Make the ''faster'' approximate (or build toward over the series of 50s) the effort level you'll reach while swimming your race. How well can you keep your focus? Hold your form? That's how well you'll be able to stay efficient in races.

The most powerful testimony I can give for the effectiveness of sensory skill practice is that I've actually seen it succeed where drill work stumbled. Despite all the wonderful things I've seen drills do for people, some swimmers just have a hard time with them. For one reason or another—poor kick, poor coordination, even anxiety about being in the water—they struggle when they drill, and unfortunately even begin to wonder if they're swimming-student material.

Of course they are. They just need a more customized curriculum. So what I do for these drill-resistant types is pull back on their drill work. We look for a minimum that just begins to cut the sensory groove for the needle, and we spend more time on the more conscious stroke modifications of sensory skill practice. They apply the same principles the drills teach, but they apply them directly and more quickly into the stroke.

Most everyone can learn the new sensations better, faster, and more clearly with drills. But if they're not working for you, sensory skill practice may jump-start your progress.

Stroke Eliminators and Swimming Golf: Two Tests of Your SSP

The whole point of sensory skill practice, of course, is not to make you *feel* better but to make you *swim* better, to build a more efficient stroke. And a more efficient stroke, you'll remember, is one that moves your body farther through the water so you need fewer of them to go any given distance. More work from less energy. Since fewer and longer strokes have been identified over and over as the consistent mark of the expert swimmer, the advantage is not merely theoretical. It's what earns medals for the competitive and personal satisfaction for the rest of us.

Fine. But how do you find out whether you're making any progress? Glad you asked. Our next two practice strategies measure just that.

Stroke Eliminators

The first is called stroke eliminators because that's just what it is— nothing fancier than simply disciplining yourself to use fewer strokes than you usually do.

It's an effective tactic Alexander Popov has used to become one of the most efficient swimmers on earth. And it can work just as well for you—even if your numbers are understandably a little different. Popov, remember, has earned the title of being untouchable in the 50-meter freestyle, swimming's version of a flat-out sprint. Race after race, he takes exactly 34 strokes to get from one end of the pool to the other. But to achieve that remarkably low count, he disciplines himself to do even better in practice, often forcing himself during 50-meter repeats to take an extremely stingy 28 strokes on each. By training his body to get by on those 28, the 34 he allows himself on race day (still three fewer than any of his rivals can manage, mind you) are a piece of cake.

If that seven-stroke spread doesn't seem exactly stunning, try this for yourself. Find a true Olympic-size pool (50 meters or 165 feet, not the bathtubs that turnpike motels love to trumpet as "Olympic size"). First, see how many strokes it takes you to swim a slow length. Next, see how many strokes it takes you to swim a fast length. A huge difference, isn't there? I thought so. You can start narrowing that down by doing a variation of a set Popov has perfected.

Its objective: to see how close he can get to his race speed without taking more than 28 strokes. He starts with a "slow" 50 meters (maybe 10 or more seconds slower than his 22-second race time), and on each successive repeat he goes a little faster. When he can't go any quicker and still hold 28 strokes, he drops back to "slow" and works his way back up the speed curve again, trying on each round to eke out a bit more speed and get ever closer to his race speed without ever exceeding his 28-stroke allotment.

Now, that's discipline. And it's discipline you can try too, using a variation of Popov's set. First, get an average stroke count for 25 yards (or whatever the length of your regular pool). Make it realistic, not what you need to do a single, perfect, well-rested length. Make it the count at the end of, say, the 27th length of a half-mile swim. You've been working awhile, you're getting tired, and your form is probably somewhere around "serviceable."

From now on, that's the number to beat, no matter how many lengths you swim. Take the pledge. Refuse, under pain of disgrace and dishonor, to take that many strokes for that distance again, for any reason.

Here's how it works. If you normally take 21 to 22 strokes per length, your mission now is to do all repeats in 19 to 20 strokes and not one more. Seems simple at first, doesn't it? You swim a series of 10 50-yard repeats, feeling fresh on the first few and easily holding the 19-to-20-stroke count. This stroke elimination's a breeze!

Then, on the second length of the fourth repeat, you head nonchalantly down the pool, take your 20th stroke, and uh-oh. How come the wall is still five yards away?

And what can you do about it? You've sworn not to take the 21st stroke, so there's only one thing to do: roll to your side and kick to the wall. Hmmmmm. Evidently this stroke elimination business will take some work after all.

So as you begin your next length, and every one from now on, you become the miser of arm turnover, keenly aware of how you *spend* every stroke, making sure that you make 20 of them stretch 25 yards. The clock is forgotten. The rival in the next lane is forgotten. The only thing that matters is how you're spending what you have to spend— which is how you learn to save. Just like real life.

Repeat after me: You're working on how *well* you get there, not how *fast*. At first, a lower stroke count will slow you down. Expect that, and don't worry about it. You'll also have to stretch and glide longer. That's okay too. Your old count was "normal" for so long that it will take some time for your body to adjust. Eventually, the lower, more efficient count will become your "new normal," and somehow, in all that obsession with strokes, your speed will have come back too while you weren't looking. As good teachers have always known, discipline teaches what indulgence never could.

Twenty strokes per 25-yard length is a meaningful benchmark for where the swimming wheat and chaff are separated. If your count is higher, don't slacken your stroke-eliminating efforts until you get there or below. When you can easily swim 25 yards in 20 strokes or less, try for 50 in 40 or less, then 75 yards in 60 strokes or less. But don't blindly add lengths to your repeats if it means taking more than 20 strokes per length. The only way to become a consistently efficient swimmer is to refuse to practice inefficient swimming.

When you can routinely swim 100 yards—four lengths—in 80 strokes or less (Tom Dolan, the American record-holder in the 1,650-yard freestyle, took 56 strokes per 100 yards while setting his mile record), you're ready to start building sets of 100-yard repeats on 15 to 30 seconds of rest. Once you can do eight to ten of those—and never take more than 80 strokes—you'll have crossed an important threshold toward swimming success. You could certainly take that stroke to a triathlon or Masters meet and show it off with pride.

So discipline yourself to count strokes nearly every length until efficiency has become habit. Then, like Popov, you can begin to trade them shrewdly for speed. Spend the fewest strokes for the most additional speed, and if you're not satisfied at the cost, try it again. Swim two or three 50-yard repeats at your lowest count. Then several more, each one a little faster, trying to reduce the "stroke cost" for each second of speed gain. Run through the cycle over and over. Get a better deal each time. Drive a hard bargain with yourself. As you master the 50-yard transaction, try it with your 100-yard repeats, which will give you a larger field on which to play the game. The game of golf. Swimming golf, that is.

SSP: What Champions Gain by Swimming Slowly

When the Russian National Swim Team spent a month at the University of South Carolina training to beat the U.S. National Team, they could hardly keep any secrets from Bill Irwin. Irwin, my first real coach when I began swimming in high school, lives in Columbia, South Carolina, and swims every day at U.S.C. So he just camped out with the Russians each morning, eyes open, notepad in hand, video camera humming.

He didn't see what he expected, Irwin admitted. Impressive swimming, yes, but not grueling nor even especially fast. ''The whole month they hardly ever broke a sweat,'' Irwin recalled. ''They swam four to five hours a day, doing endless sets of easy freestyle repeats with a half-catchup stroke.'' (See the hand-swapping drill in Chapter 7).

Easy, perhaps, but exacting.

Why, Irwin asked the Russian coach, did they do all that work on this exaggerated stroke? Because, came the answer, one of world champion Alexander Popov's big advantages was his habit of always having one hand in front of his head to lengthen his body. So the coach wanted all of his freestylers to make that a habit too, and he knew it didn't come naturally. They would simply have to make it natural, ''burn it into the nervous system'' by running that loop over and over for hours a day until each swimmer's nervous system *owned* it. Whatever the Russian

continued

term for it may be, they devoted that entire month to practicing one form of sensory skill practice—hand-swapping—with extraordinary patience. No question that it came before any hard or fast swimming.

Too bad one of the most gifted freestylers in the U.S. wasn't there to watch. On the West Coast for a Total Immersion workshop, I had a chance to watch him train for 30 minutes, knowing that he's raced with the world's best, even swimming on world-record-setting relays, but that those great swims have eluded him for the past few years. He's even talked of quitting, though still years short of his prime.

So I watched, curious, as he did a series of sprints alternating with easy recovery lengths. And what do you know? On each sprint, his body stretched out long and efficient. But on every easy length, he lapsed into sloppy form. Thinking only of physical recovery, he didn't realize his easy laps were also training his nervous system to lapse into inefficiency whenever he got tired. In his mind, the hard effort—working the physiology—was the valuable part of the workout. But his careless training of his nervous system was completely undermining the aerobic work.

His slump no longer surprises me.

Swimming Golf

It's possible to get too carried away with this business of eliminating strokes when you're down to such a triumphantly tiny number of strokes that you're taking forever to get to the other end. Clever types can also figure out a way to cheat the stroke-eliminator system so the numbers are better but the swimming is not—say by gliding or kicking half a length after pushoff. If the real point of all these efficiency gains is swimming faster, you want to know whether that's happening. Well, just tee up for some swimming golf, the second strategy for increasing your stroke efficiency.

You don't need a club membership or a taste for Scotch, and the rules are simple. For a given distance, count your strokes and add that to your time in seconds. A reasonably good swimmer can usually swim the two lengths of a 50-yard repeat in 40 strokes and 40 seconds. That's a score of 80. (Notice how conveniently the scores on 50-yard repeats approximate those on a golf round.) A "duffer" can usually aim for a score of 90, serious swimmers might be in the low 60s. Repeats of 50 yards are best because the numbers are easy to work with.

Always lower your score by reducing stroke count first and *later* by trying to swim faster. Just a few rounds should be eye-opening. You'll be amazed how quickly a bit more effort can add a lot more strokes. If those strokes don't translate into enough speed to lower your total score, you know right away how wasteful you've been. Remember, speed equals stroke rate (SR) multiplied by stroke length (SL), and just about everyone has enough SR. It's your SL that needs work. Your golf score will be an unerring measure of how well you're using SL to create speed. Fore!

We've finally finished drawing the Total Immersion learning curve. You now understand that technique, not sweat or muscle, is the foundation for the serious swimming improvement you're about to embark on. It started with finding out how your body *really* moves through the water, the quickest and most dramatic changes you can make to improve that, the drills that start those changes happening, and finally how to practice the smoother and more satisfying swimming that the drills are helping you achieve so that your new stroke becomes second nature.

Now it's time to get to the pool and start putting your new plan to work—getting fit by practicing proper technique. In Chapter 8, we'll get suited up, onto the deck, and wet. It's time to start your "workouts"—the new way.

Enough classroom talk. Let's get to work.

You know by now that skill drills are the fastest way to make dramatic improvements in your swimming stroke, since they erase bad habits and build new and better ones. In the Total Immersion system, as we've said, drills break up the complex motions of skillful swimming into small pieces that are easily mastered one by one, then gradually reassemble them into a new, more comfortable and faster swim stroke.

Each drill builds on the one before it, so in the beginning try to get comfortable with one drill before moving on to the next. Use the illustrations which appear at the end of each drill for guidance. You're on your way to becoming your own best coach, and as you progress from the individual drills to drill-swim and into sen-

sory skill practice, you'll become better able to pinpoint for yourself techniques that need more work—and the particular drills that will accomplish them for you. When you've reached that level, you can repeat any drill you might need at any time as a refresher. I do it all the time. But in the beginning, take them one after the other.

The students in my weekend workshops are given a concentrated introduction to all the drills in just two days. While it's possible to learn the rudiments that quickly while receiving expert instruction, it takes longer for the muscles to fully understand than it does the mind. So I recommend to them that, following the workshop, they spend several weeks to several months doing drills almost exclusively, and that they give the body time to patiently absorb their many lessons.

This chapter is broken up into four lessons, each lesson made up of highly complementary and naturally sequenced drills. Since you'll be learning without benefit of a coach standing over you, I suggest you try spending three to four hours of swim time, spread out over numerous visits to the pool, mastering just one lesson before moving on to the next. As you move from Lesson One to Lesson Two, start each session with 10 to 15 minutes of review of the moves you've already mastered. Use the same review steps as you segue from Lesson Two to Lesson Three. Over a period of several weeks to several months of concentrated practice, your body should become ready to begin integrating a variety of drills and lessons into a single practice session. The learning curve will be different for every swimmer, so my best advice is tune in to your own body. It will tell you loud and clear how comfortable it's becoming with each new set of skills.

Lesson One: The Secret of Getting Balanced

You'll swim better because: Nothing slows you down more than hips and legs dragging along behind you. Even if you're in mediocre physical shape and have arm movements that could best be described as merely serviceable, you'll pick up speed fast if you first just get those legs and hips up where they belong. Next, you'll need to learn how to keep that body balance through the full swimming stroke, which constantly threatens to throw you off in little ways with big consequences.

Drill 1: Pressing Your Buoy

The drill problem: Hips and legs that sink

The drill result: You'll instinctively redistribute your weight so you balance your body from head to toe, letting the water do the work.

First, get your head on straight—in a manner of speaking. Imagine a line running from the top of your head along your spine to your hips. As long as your head is on that head-spine line, its weight can help counterbalance your hips and legs at the other end, essentially levering them up like a seesaw. But lift your head even a little bit from the water and the opposite happens: Down go the hips.

Step one is to flutter kick, face down, arms pressed lightly at your sides. (Don't concern yourself with arm movement now; your only goal is to keep them out of the way.) Kick gently and with straight though supple legs. Don't be labored or splashy. As you kick, you'll press your buoy into the water to lever your hips and legs toward the surface. It's simple to do. Just lean on the area between your chin and sternum. Another way to think of it is trying to push your upper chest toward the bottom of the pool. The object is to get your butt-cheeks to "kiss" the surface, though the motion probably sounds unnatural and even silly until you try it—and the hips bob right up. I've seen it happen time and time again.

Don't use churning legs to *prop* your hips up, or your lower back muscles, which should be relaxed, to *hold* them up. Simply lean on your chin and sternum and *release* your hips to the surface. (Careful. Don't be so enthusiastic that your hips pop right through the surface. And don't bury your head.) A balanced body means a neutral line from head to hips, no bend at the waist, no sway in the back. Have a spotter check you to be sure. Practice kicking short distances—10 to 25 yards—this way.

Oh, yes: you'll have to breathe at some point, though the easier your kick, the less often you'll need to. When you do, breathe by moving your chin forward until your mouth just clears the water. Of course, your hips will drop as you do, so press your buoy to rebalance as quickly as possible after your breath.

Experiment. Ease the pressure a little and feel your hips drop a lot.

Skill Drills: Time to Get Started — — — — — — — —

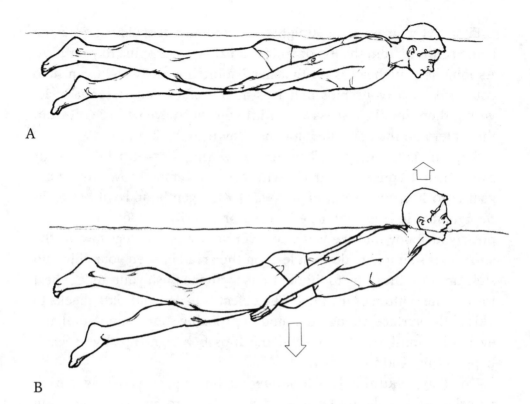

A

B

Reapply it, and up they come again. Kick a length or two, adjusting all the way, until you know exactly how much pressure it takes to get it right.

Once you've got it, hips just skimming the surface with ease, alternate a drill length with a swim length. On both, concentrate on having the same feeling of pressing your chest into the water—I call it *swimming downhill.* Do your hips feel lighter? I'll bet they do. Is it easier to kick? I told you so. More of your body's weight is being supported by the water. As you're pressing your lighter, upper half down, the water is lifting up your heavier, lower half. That's a good tradeoff, since it lets you swim more relaxed.

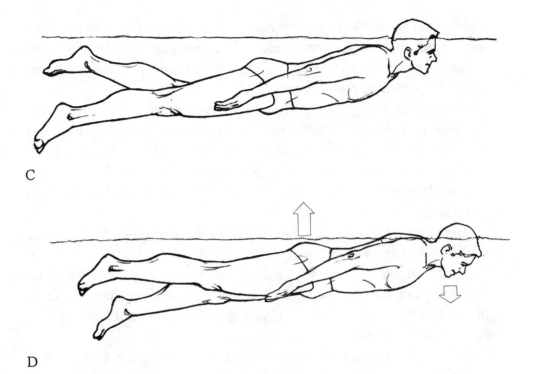

C

D

Drill 2: Balancing on Your Back

The drill problem: Unless you can balance in almost any position, you won't be able to breathe easily.

The drill result: Learn what balance feels like upside-down, so you can eventually keep it through all 360 degrees and the simple act of breathing can no longer throw you off.

In freestyle, the most common cause of poor balance is turning your head to breathe and leaving your body behind. Turn your head without rolling your body at all, or even just a little before your hips roll, and you lose your balance—hips drop—or alignment—hips sway side to side and legs fishtail—with every single breath. Lift your head even

Skill Drills: Time to Get Started — — — — — — — —

slightly and what also happens? Right. Down go the hips. None of this occurs, however, when your *body* rolls to breathe and the head just comes along for the ride. So the next drill and the few after that teach you how to breathe *and* stay balanced.

Start on your back. True, you swim freestyle more or less face down, but you want to learn balance on all sides of your body because your sense of balance should be global. After all, we said "more or less" face down. Actually, once you've begun to build a true Total Immersion stroke, you'll see that swimming freestyle face down is something of a misnomer.

First, kick easily on your back. Tuck your chin slightly, as if you were holding an orange under it. You'll still press your buoy to keep your hips up, but now it's the back of your head and your upper spine that you push into the water. Feel your hips and thighs bob closer to the surface. You should feel as if you were lying on your back in bed, not sitting in a chair.

Kick with your hands at your sides and your shoulders slightly rounded, knees and toes just under the surface, not breaking through. (Press that buoy—especially the back of your head!) If you have to scull your hands lightly to keep moving, that's okay. Practice for several lengths until your balance feels natural and easy. When it does, you're ready to roll.

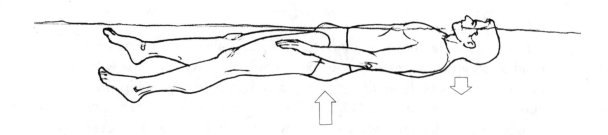

Drill 3: Rolling to Breathe

The drill problem: Turn your head to breathe and you'll throw your carefully balanced body off every time.

The drill result: Learn instead to roll all at once, staying balanced, so your head turns along with your body instead of by itself like a periscope. Result: no more sinking hips every time you breathe.

Start face down, kicking gently in a balanced position. This time when you need a breath, don't lift your chin. Instead, just roll over onto your back—rolling to the left or right, whatever feels more natural—keeping your arms at your sides, all at once, like a log.

The secret to staying balanced in this one is to make sure your head doesn't get going too soon. So we'll work on eliminating the stubborn habit most heads seem to have of wanting to go first. We'll make it go last for awhile. As you begin to roll, keep your head still and your face pressed lightly into the water until your shoulder nearly touches your chin. Only then will you let your head follow. The more slowly you roll, the more control you'll have.

When you settle onto your back, kick, breathing easily. Remember to tuck your chin; remember to keep pressing your buoy. After you catch your breath, you can roll face down again. Same rule applies; Keep the back of your head fixed and pressed in as you begin rolling your torso until your shoulder nears your chin. Then your head can follow.

Practice a length or two, rolling from one position to the other and back. Kick face down until you need a breath. Roll to your back to breathe. Roll face down again after you've caught your breath. Beware: Wait too long to roll for breath and you'll need air so urgently you'll either jerk your head up or whip it around too fast. Either way, your balance will be gone.

Skill Drills: Time to Get Started — — — — — — — —

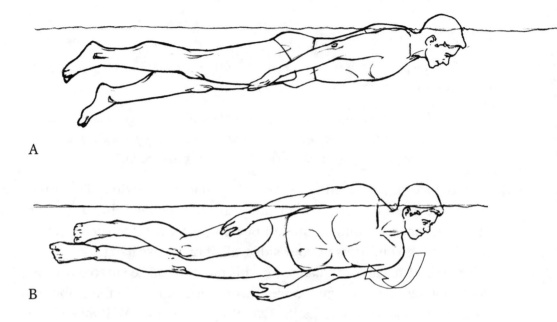

A

B

Practice this until the coordination begins to feel natural. When it does, we need to take one more step, and that is to work on keeping steady buoy pressure at all "points of the compass." That way you'll be balanced not just on your front and back but through the whole roll.

You do this with a *moving* buoy, which simply means that although you keep pressing your buoy, the spot you press changes. Starting face down—as you certainly know by now—you lean on your sternum to keep your hips up. But what keeps them from going down as you roll toward your side? Same thing. Except that the pressure has to gradually move from your chest across to your shoulder and finally onto your back. You're always pressing into the water the point that's closest to the bottom of the pool. Same thing as you roll back.

Practice rolling both clockwise and counterclockwise until you feel

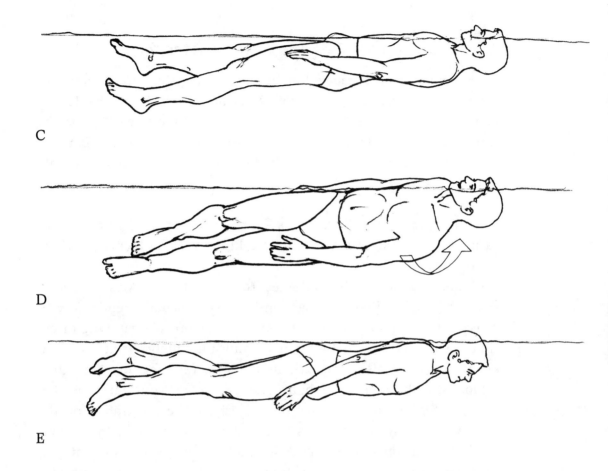

C

D

E

balanced and stable at all times. Roll to your back to breathe. Then roll face down again. Press your buoy in every position.

And that's all there is to basic balance. It's not difficult to learn, but it can be kind of slippery and hard to hold onto at first. So plan on using these drills as a warmup for the first few lengths of your workouts. It's a little refresher course that will bring your muscles' balance memory back quickly.

Skill Drills: Time to Get Started — — — — — — —

Lesson Two: The Longer, Faster You

You'll swim better because: Remember Froude, the famous naval architect from Chapter 3? Longer boats are faster boats, he found. Longer swimmers are too, as we said then. But too few of us use the techniques that make us "taller" and speedier in the water. Let's fix that right now: Time to turn your body into a long, balanced, smoothly rolling vessel.

These drills are not difficult, but if you've got an efficient kick they'll be easier still. So take time out and do a little "vertical kicking" first to get you ready.

Runners and many other athletes frequently have ankles that won't flex very much. When that happens, the knee usually bends to compensate, making your swimming kick look more like running or cycling. Not efficient, not effective, and ultimately tiring. Vertical kicking in deep water is a nearly infallible exercise for correcting that.

Float straight up and down, arms folded across your chest, head at the surface, mouth just above the water; see the illustration on the next page. Using the muscles at the top of your thigh, move your whole leg like a pendulum. Kick with a leg that's nearly straight, just supple enough to respond to water pressure. Practice several times for 10 to 15 seconds, resting (tread water or hold the wall) between each. Then kick with the same action on our next drills.

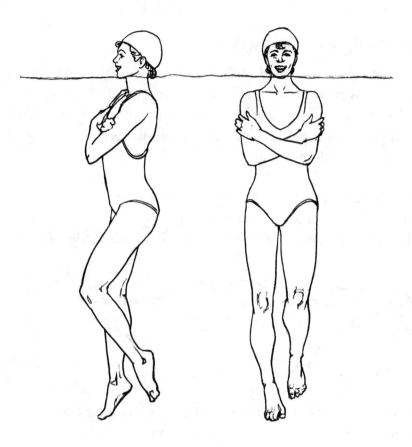

Drill 4: Both Balanced and Longer

The drill problem: When you extend your arms to make your body longer, which is good, you have to learn how to balance a longer body.

The drill result: You'll be able to balance—and get longer at the same time—without losing your place.

Skill Drills: Time to Get Started — — — — — — — —

Try This Before You Get Into the Pool:

Stand with both arms extended in front of your shoulders. Place one hand and wrist over the other, elbows hyperextended. Then squeeze your shoulders against your jaw while looking at your hands. That's the position in which we'll kick now and to which we'll return after each stroke in the next few drills.

Stretch your arms in front of you as you will in your new swimming stroke, and you'll feel the sensation of leaning into the water less in your chin and much more in your sternum. It will take a little getting used to.

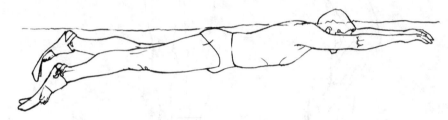

A

If your kick doesn't propel you very well, this is a good time to slip on a pair of fins. Kick gently, pressing your buoy as before, but this

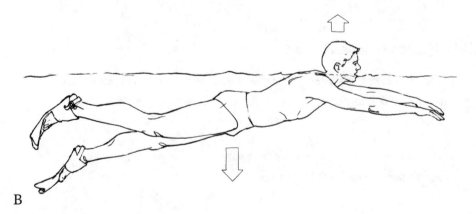

B

C

time with your arms extended. Hold them out in front, hand over hand, elbows locked (if you find you need to scull your hands a bit, that's okay too), shoulders squeezed against your jaw. Look toward your hands, not at the pool bottom, and kick a full length, concentrating on pushing your weight down on your sternum and keeping your hips near the surface.

When you need a breath, move your chin forward until your mouth just clears. Notice your hips sink. Lift them back to the surface as quickly as possible by leaning downhill with your chest. Practice several lengths this way, trying to keep your body more balanced and stable each time.

Drill 5: Balanced, Longer, and Rolling: The Single-Arm

The drill problem: You can balance and you can breathe, but how do you do both?

The drill result: Roll-and-breathe 101—the beginnings of balanced head movement.

Now that you understand how to rebalance the body after each breath, let's learn to take that breath by rolling the body, not by lifting or turning the head. Start kicking in the same arms-extended posi-

Skill Drills: Time to Get Started — — — — — — — —

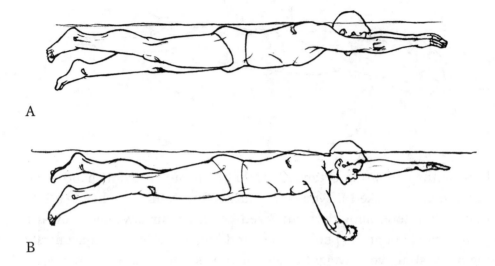

A

B

tion as in Drill 4: streamlined, balanced, and stable. This time, when you need to breathe, do it by stroking one arm and rolling to your side as you do. Start with the side you're more comfortable breathing on.

Here's the action: Pull your hand straight down the centerline of your body. As your hand approaches your hips, roll them completely out of the way so your belly button faces the sidewall. As you roll to your side, your head simply moves with your body (keep your chin and sternum aligned) until your mouth clears the water. After you've got that breath, roll back to your balanced face-down position and cover your extended hand with your stroking hand again.

You're back where you were in the previous drill. Press your buoy and kick easily until you feel balanced and stable. When you need to breathe again, repeat. Continue for a full length, working on the same side.

Next, do a length with the opposite arm. If you're stroking with the

C

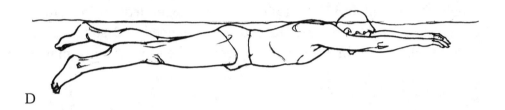

D

left arm this time, your right stays extended, helping with balance and direction. It also gives you a target for the left hand to return to each time.

Practice a few more lengths—going down the pool with one arm, coming back with the other—to get coordinated. If this is your first time breathing to your less-natural side—and everybody has one of those—it may take a little more time getting comfortable in that direction. Be patient.

Drill 6: Balanced, Longer, and Rolling: Alternating Single-Arm (Catchup)

The drill problem: You've learned the basic moves of rolling the body to each side to breathe. Now we have to turn that into a smooth, coordinated right-left-right-left pattern that you'll use when swimming.

The drill result: You'll roll smoothly from side to side, with less drag and fresher muscles.

Skill Drills: Time to Get Started — — — — — — — —

Catchup is the same as single-arm, but this time you breathe to alternating sides—a right-arm stroke-and-breath follows a left-arm stroke-and-breath and so on, breathing every stroke. The idea is to teach your body to roll in smooth symmetry from one side to the other, which not only reduces drag but puts more power into your stroke.

Push off the wall and kick face down, arms extended out in front as before, pressing your buoy until you feel balanced and stable. Now stroke the right arm directly down the centerline of your body, maybe

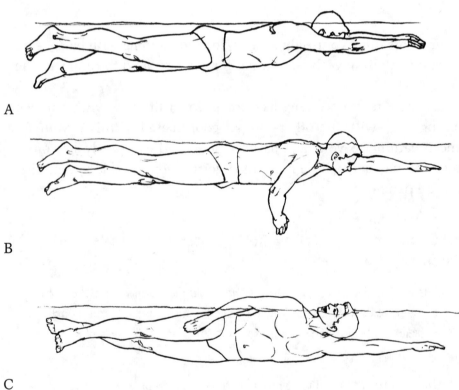

A

B

C

18 inches deep. As your hand approaches your hips, roll to the side to breathe so your belly button faces the wall. After your breath, recover the right arm and roll back to the original streamlined catchup position and press your buoy until your body is balanced and stable. Good. Your reward for this balancing act? You get to take a breath on the left. Continue down the pool, alternating a right arm stroke-and-breath with a left, and *rolling* with each.

Practice the basic moves until they become comfortable, usually in

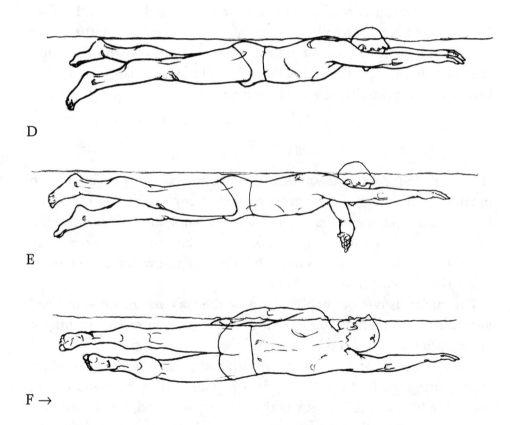

D

E

F →

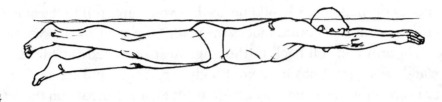

G

about five minutes or maybe four to six 25-yard repeats for swimmers at my workshops. Keep it simple for now. Think about just two things: 1. Don't stroke and breathe until your body feels balanced and stable. 2. Get your breath by rolling your hips (torso and head naturally go with them) out of the way of your hand as it strokes down the center-line. Is your belly button facing the sidewall as you finish each stroke? Good, you've got it. Time for the next step.

Staying Balanced as You Roll

Have you felt your body sink a few inches each time you roll to breathe even though you're pressing your buoy for all you're worth? Don't get discouraged; you've got plenty of company. It's not complicated to fix, but it's important to fix. Remember, the more your body sinks, the harder it becomes to push it through the water. So you want to get rid of "that sinking feeling."

The culprit is two old habits affecting the way you move your head as you roll to breathe: You're still lifting it, or you're still turning it before you move your body, or both.

Let's fix the second one first. Simply make sure your head doesn't move during the first third of each pull. Wait until your hand passes your chin to start rolling your body so that your head, torso, and hips move all at once. Pretend someone is watching as you go down the pool. They should see your head and butt move together each and every roll. Practice this until you don't have to concentrate too hard to make it happen. You'll need that concentration for the next step—eliminating head-lift.

Raise your head even a little, you see, and you set off a chain reaction. Something now has to support your head's weight, and the job falls squarely onto your extended arm. The weight of those 15 pounds will instantly drive your hand down and back—making you a shorter swimmer. So do this instead: As you roll to breathe, press your ear (or your cap if you're wearing one) into the shoulder of the extended arm so all of your head's weight is buoyed up by the water. Now that forward arm is free to do a more important job—making you longer and more slippery. And always always always press that buoy as you roll, everything from the top of your cap to the bottom of your rib cage. Practice for five to ten minutes until you can do this well on every stroke.

We've saved the best for last—the main benefit of this drill, which is what I call the weightless arm. Sounds like a magic trick, I know, but it's actually a way of knowing whether or not you're as streamlined as you should be.

If you're pressing your head and buoy into the water properly as you roll, you should quickly notice the most desirable result of this drill: Your extended hand feels weightless. And in a sense, it is. The water is now buoying up the weight of your head and body, as it should be. Make this work for you by concentrating on thrusting the fingertips of your extended hand toward the far end of the pool. You'll feel taller each time you roll to breathe, and you already know what that means. Your body slips through the water faster and goes a little farther with each stroke.

Prove that's what's happening. Take a little time out from the drills

Skill Drills: Time to Get Started — — — — — — — — —

now, and begin weaving the threads of these new and separate skills into the fabric of your improved swim stroke. You've already changed for the better. It's time to see how.

Alternate drill and swim lengths. On the drill length, practice Drill 6 until the feeling of a long, balanced body sliding easily forward becomes vivid and consistent. On swim lengths, use simpler cues: 1. Look first for the feeling you're swimming downhill, with light hips and relaxed legs. Press that moving buoy along a band that goes from one armpit to the other, across your chest, as you roll. 2. Feel your *weightless arm* as you reach forward (like stretching for something on a high shelf) to extend your bodyline before each stroke. On non-breathing strokes, you should feel the shoulder of your reaching arm pressing against your jawline. On breathing strokes, press your ear or cap into your shoulder. Ideally, your stroke will eventually feel exactly like the drill. For now, you just want them as close as possible. Try to swim at least the first few strokes without breathing so you can feel how your body responds to your drill changes. Then keep your new rhythm as you blend in your breathing pattern.

One more caution: sometimes the drills do such a good job of creating "muscle amnesia," forcing out old stroke habits, that you actually forget you're swimming now—you're still instinctively touching hands in front and breathing to both sides as you did on the drill length. Take a moment before each swim length to mentally rehearse how you'd like your stroke to feel and to remind yourself: This is swimming; no catchup, and no breathing on every stroke.

Lesson Three: Side-swimming—Perfectly Balanced

You'll swim better because: You glide most easily in the water on your side, so you need to spend more time there.

If you were a boat instead of a swimmer, as we said in Chapter 3, you'd have two choices: Be like a barge or be like an America's Cup yacht. Barges plow wastefully along flat to the water, pushing everything in front of them. America's Cup yachts slice neatly through with a minimum of resistance and fuss. Obviously, you're not reading this book to become a barge.

So let's go over it once again: The most hydrodynamically perfect position that your body can be in is balanced, lying on your side, one arm extended for length. Not so very different from the way fish do it. The longer you can glide in that position between strokes, the farther and faster your body will travel.

Unfortunately, nature didn't set up our nervous system to feel comfortable imitating fish. It's a skill we acquire. So far, we've zeroed in on balance in the prone position and while rolling side to side. Now it's time for the next step, mastering "side-lying balance." It's the only way you'll ever be comfortable rolling *all the way* to each side, then *staying* there for maximum glide. Instinct says, "Get flat again as soon as you can." We've got to reprogram instinct.

As we do, you'll find out which is your "chocolate" side and which is your "vanilla" (or perhaps your pistachio versus your rum raisin—in any case, your favorite and less-than-favorite sides). Years of studying underwater videotapes of swimmers have shown me that nearly

Skill Drills: Time to Get Started — — — — — — — — —

everyone has one side on which they balance more instinctively. Mine is the left, which I therefore call chocolate for my favorite flavor. If you have a chocolate side, this series of drills will reveal it and allow you to give a little extra attention to your other side.

So let's learn side-lying balance.

Drill 7: Slide on Your Side

The drill problem: Your body in the water glides best on its side, but it instinctively avoids the position.

The drill result: Once the body learns it can in fact balance and breathe in this somewhat foreign posture, it stops fighting you and stays there as long as you want it to.

Step one is to become comfortable in a basically alien-feeling position, to stay balanced while kicking on your side. This is a brand-new sensation, admittedly harder to get used to than the others. So even if you haven't used fins thus far, you may want to slip on a pair now.

Kick one length lying on, say, your left side. Your left arm is extended overhead, right arm lying on your side. Turn your chin just far enough toward your right shoulder that your mouth is clear of the water and you can breathe comfortably. Your right hip and shoulder should point straight up, and your kick should be compact.

As you seem to be coming close to swallowing half the pool, remember this: Balancing in this position goes against every instinct you've got. You must keep your head and rib cage pressed firmly into the water. You'll be tempted to lift your head to breathe, and who can blame you? But do that and your hips will drop—end of delicate balance. Practice, practice, practice—one length on one side, next length

Dry-Land Slide on Your Side. Do this at home first.

Before heading to the pool, try this. Lie on one side with your bottom arm extended, forming a straight line from fingertips to toes. Your top arm is resting along your side. Press your lower shoulder into the floor and press the back of your head into the bicep of your extended arm. Turn your head so your nose points upward (as if toward the air). Now you're in the same side-lying balance position you'll be practicing in the water.

  Do this often enough to make it feel natural. At the pool, try it on deck as a preworkout refresher. Notice that if you lift your head even slightly off your shoulder, you can feel your hips press into the floor. In the water, of course, they'll just plain sink.

on the other—until you're comfortable with balance on both the left side and the right.

Skill Drills: Time to Get Started — — — — — — — —

Drill 8: Slide-Front-Slide

The drill problem: Now you can balance pretty comfortably on your left side and on your right, but you don't know how to roll from one to the other while staying balanced.

The drill result: Link the two positions with a "balance pause" in the middle.

Start kicking on your right side, right arm extended, left arm lying on your side. After half a length, slowly slide the left hand up your hip, almost like you were taking your hand out of your pocket, then drag your thumb up your side as if you were pulling a zipper up. As your hand passes your face, roll back toward the face-down position, and cover the right hand with your left as you roll onto your stomach, just like catchup.

A

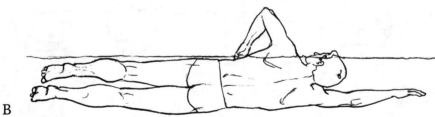

B

Pause for balance, then stroke with the right hand and roll onto your left side. Balance in that position, just as you did on the right side, and kick to the wall. On the next length repeat the action, but start out on your left side and roll to your right.

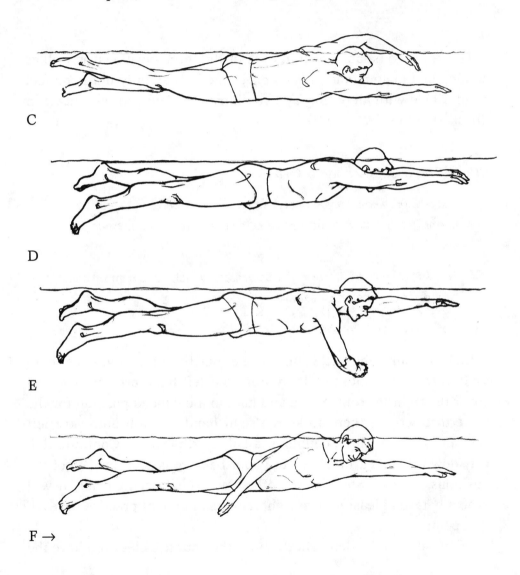

C

D

E

F →

G

The key is to balance well in each of the three positions, as well as coming in and going out of each one. Practice patiently until you feel comfortable with all of this, and you'll have earned your certificate in "basic side-to-side."

Drill 9: Three-Count Slide & Glide

The drill problem: As you speed up body roll closer and closer to normal tempo, it gets harder to hold your carefully rehearsed body position.

The drill result: You'll learn how to gradually pick up steam without falling off the "balance highwire."

Note: Refer to illustration for Drill 8.

Kick on your right side, counting one–one thousand, two–one thousand, three–one thousand, then drag your left hand up your side and cover the right in front. Pause and kick in a balanced position for the same three-count, then stroke the right hand and roll onto your left side and kick for three counts in a balanced position. Continue that way down the pool. Practice until your balance is good in each of the positions. As with some of the other more challenging drills, it will probably take at least four to eight lengths of patient practice to reach that point.

Whatever you do, don't shortchange the count. Unless you have the reflexes of an Olympic skier, you'll need every moment of it not only to highlight and correct balance errors but also to give yourself time to think about all the new movements in this drill. As with the catchup drill, we'll continue with this drill for a while because there's so much to think about. We'll cover the points one at a time to keep the concentration manageable.

Right off, you probably noticed one nagging problem: After rolling to your side, your balance is usually off again. You have to take time consciously fixing it by pressing your buoy. Ultimately, of course, you want to roll in and roll right out again with no pause for repair work, so let's go back and borrow one of the tricks from the catchup drill. Before each stroke, use your three-count pause in the prone position (both arms extended and streamlined, remember, and buoy pressed for balance), not just to ensure that your body is balanced before you roll but for a quick rehearsal for the coordination that keeps you balanced as you do.

It's a 1-2-3 prestroke checkoff, and you do it *every* time:

1. Head moves with torso—never before. ☑
2. Starting each stroke, nothing moves until hand passes head. ☑
3. When it does, everything from head to hips rolls at once. ☑

Practice several lengths of three-count slide & glide putting all the concentration you can muster into making sure your head and butt roll together. Full three counts in all three positions, please. And press that head and armpit into the water as you roll. Put all your weight on your buoy, don't lift your head at all, and you'll feel that wonderful, weightless arm extending out in front, virtually pulling you along just a few inches below the surface as you roll onto your side and your body feels long, streamlined, a quicksilver yacht slicing easily through the water. Just keep practicing patiently until you feel exactly that way.

Drill 10: Power Surge & Slide

The drill problem: All the drills so far reduce drag. How do I also add power?

The drill result: Discovering that better propulsion has little to do with arm strength. It all starts in the hips.

Note: Refer to illustration for Drill 8.

So far, you've worked hard just to get drag down to an absolute minimum and wring the most "miles per gallon" from the horsepower you've got. But there are ways of boosting the horsepower too.

To start, think of the slide & glide drill as having a double-barreled effect. The first conserves your momentum by letting you glide as far as possible between strokes. The second creates more surge or momentum for you to conserve in the first place.

Let's get to that second part right now, since it's built into what we've been doing all along in catchup and slide & glide. The good news is that moving forward more powerfully comes from simple improvements in coordination, not from lots of grueling training.

When you roll your head, torso, and hips as a unit, you not only balance yourself, you also tap more power by essentially connecting powerful back muscles directly up to your arm. Using hip and back muscles to snap the torso onto its side adds far more power to your pull than you could ever muster from arm muscles alone. And moving everything from your head to your hips at the same time gets the maximum amount of mass moving in the same direction.

You've got a head start on this one. All that work, for so many lengths, to move everything—head, torso, hips—at once when you stroke has also started you on the road to a more powerful stroke. Now you can increase that power simply by moving your hips with more snap, rolling the body more crisply to its side. The arms and hands no longer have to pull or yank on the water; they simply hold onto it as body roll drives the arm back.

Once again, you start by making sure your hips, not your head, move first. Make it happen by keeping your head still as you begin pulling back. After the arm has begun its pull, the head and torso move all at once, as though they were glued to the hips, and the whole body rolls like a log. Do it right, with a more serious spin of your midsection, and you'll feel a new surge of power at the end of each stroke. Your arms aren't tired, so where did your new power center come from? Right—the hips.

Add yet more snap to hip roll and you'll feel an even more powerful surge. Don't struggle or start flailing. Try too hard and before you know it you'll probably have sent your head whipping around on its own, bleeding power rather than building it. Keep your movement smooth and spare. Remember, more might comes through carefully synchronized movement of your whole body mass than from tiring muscular effort.

The movement is simple: Pause in the prone catchup position, get balanced and stable, do the 1-2-3 prestroke checkoff, then *stroke* and snap-roll the body to its side. Balance and . . . enjoy the ride! As you feel your momentum slow, bring your upper arm forward, return to the prone catchup position, and repeat with the other arm. Hold the three counts in each position to savor each movement.

As with all the other drills, practice power surge & slide for several lengths. Start each one concentrating on the result you're looking for —using your whole body to drive your arm back. Once the coordination feels consistent, add a little more snap to your hips. Dial it up gradually until you begin to feel a slight loss of control or smoothness, then practice just below that threshold.

If it seems to you like slide & glide—and its variations—is probably

Skill Drills: Time to Get Started — — — — — — — —

the most valuable player of swim drills, you're right. There's nothing important it doesn't touch: improved balance at all points in the rotation, coordination of head and body roll for breathing, more stroking power using body roll to drive armstroke, and a longer and better-balanced body in the side-lying position.

You've come a long way already. Now it's time to work all these new skills further into your stroke by alternating slide & glide and swimming lengths. The fastest way to do that is to:

1. Go down the pool using the three-count slide & glide, concentrating mainly on perfect balance in all three positions as well as when you're shifting between them. Then, on the return swim length, focus on swimming downhill, reaching with a weightless arm, or rolling more than usual from side to side. (You'll probably add a few more degrees of roll to each side if you think about pointing your belly button at the sidewall on every stroke.) No need to exaggerate. Try to keep it feeling reasonably natural.

Pick one sensation at a time and do it well, rather than trying to get everything right with less than brilliant success.

2. Go down the pool using three-count slide & glide, concentrating on creating maximum surge with perfect head-torso-hip roll coordination and strong but smooth hip-snap. Swim back fixing on putting more snap into your hip rotation. As I suggested earlier, for best results, don't breathe for the first six to eight strokes, and keep your head perfectly still while your hips roll rhythmically from side to side. This way it will be easier to teach your hips to move independently of your head and to feel a *hip rhythm* developing—and to maintain it as you blend in your breathing pattern.

Your whole sense of stroke rhythm should be in your midsection. This is true inside-out swimming—swimming that starts where it ought to start, in the midsection—and these are two of the best ways to learn to make hip roll the source of your swimming power and rhythm.

Lesson Four—for Experts: the Total Immersion Stroke Graduate School

You'll swim better because: Face down is now out, and stroke timing becomes much more demanding and precise. Translation: even less drag, even better propulsion. But don't bother with these fine points until you get your undergraduate degree first.

When it comes to hitting all the high points of efficient swimming, as we've said, the slide & glide drills are nearly perfect. Nearly. They have two shortcomings, important only to the swimmer who's already mastered the most important fundamentals and is now looking for final stroke-polishing. You see, slide & glide drills involve spending time flat on your stomach—hydrodynamic heresy because of all that drag—and they never quite teach you the precise timing for hand-swapping. That's the trick in front-quadrant swimming of bringing your recovering arm back into the water at just the moment your stroking arm gets started so you're always as tall as you can be, as we explained in Chapter 3.

The two advanced drills here bring the stroke to its highest polish by adding those last two pieces of the puzzle, teaching your body to roll from one side directly to the other, and keying you in to just the right timing for swapping your hands in front of your head. Know, however, that each requires powerful coordination to be done well. And, like any drill, if you don't do them well they won't do much for you in return. So make sure you've got all the others down cold before spending time with these postgrad "honors courses."

Skill Drills: Time to Get Started — — — — — — — — — —

Drill 11: Postgraduate Slide on Your Side

This is a simple variation on Drill 7, and it in turn preps you for Drill 12.

You already know the first part. That's where you start kicking in a balanced position on your side, pressing your buoy, and pressing the back of your head into the shoulder of your extended arm, face turned to the side for air. Here's the difference. After kicking several yards, turn your head until your chin touches the shoulder of the extended arm and you're looking forward at your extended hand. Your body doesn't change position so much as one degree. A few yards later, turn your head again to get a breath. Alternate several times between face in and face out, moving only your head as you glide along, perfectly balanced, on your side. Practice until you can turn your head in and out with no change in your body position. Then you're ready to go on to Advanced Slide & Glide.

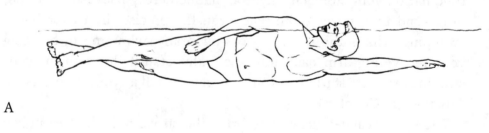

A

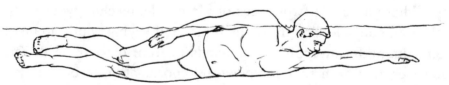

B

Drill 12: Advanced (Post-Postgraduate) Slide & Glide

Advanced Slide & Glide is similar to Three-Count Slide & Glide (Drill 9) but you eliminate the catchup position in front of your head.

Kick, balanced, on one side. Next, turn your head forward to the extended arm, pause for just a beat (one–one thousand), then recover the trailing arm. Keep the leading arm in place until your trailing hand reaches your head, then stroke and roll right over to the other side. Pause to balance, and repeat.

Let's try it. You're kicking on, say, your right side, right arm out in front. Turn your head forward until your chin just touches your right shoulder, then pause looking at your right hand. Okay, now "recover" the left arm (bring it forward), and just as your left hand passes your ear and before it gets into the water, stroke the right hand and roll directly to your left side, just as your left hand stretches into your front quadrant. Kick on your left side in a balanced position for a count of three, face turned to the right for air, head pressed into your

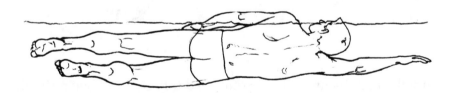

A

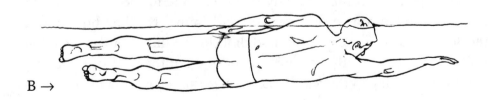

B →

Skill Drills: Time to Get Started — — — — — — — —

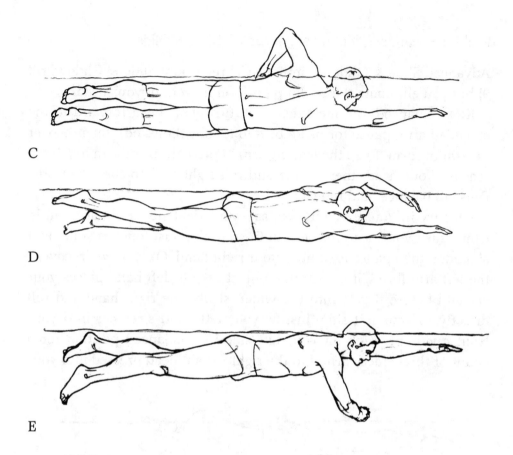

C

D

E

left shoulder for balance. Turn your head forward and begin the cycle again.

And what have you learned from all this? Two things: 1. It's taught you the feeling of rolling directly from one side to the other with no pause in the face-down position, and 2. Timing. Not just how to use the leading arm to keep your bodyline long while you recover the trailing arm, but exactly how long to leave it out there. If your leading hand isn't waiting in the front quadrant as the recovering hand enters

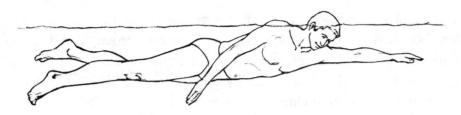

F

G

the water, you're letting your bodyline grow short on every stroke. That's no way to get fast and slippery with less effort. It's all in the timing, and this drill is the easiest way to learn that.

So there they are, a dozen drills designed to quickly clean out the cobwebs of your plodding old stroke and replace them with sound new reflexes that give you power and zip, efficiency and enjoyment. But as useful as the drills are, they can't do the job all by themselves. They may build a new stroke for you step by step, but final assembly comes from actually using the stroke—just as you have to break in a brand-new car for all its parts to get used to working smoothly together. That's where drill-and-swim sequences (Chapter 6) and sensory skill practice (Chapter 7) come in. But you'll be a better—and smarter—swimmer if you give yourself a full refresher course (a reread of those chapters) now that you've got the drills under your belt.

That's the beauty of Total Immersion swimming skills. No matter

Skill Drills: Time to Get Started — — — — — — — — —

how good you already are, you can probably get better. No matter how hopeless you think you might be, you can improve. It's all in your skills and how willing you are to practice them. You can do that—and see results—for a lifetime. Can any other sport—or any other way of swimming—make that claim?

PART TWO

Training versus Trying:
Finally, a Smarter
Path to Fitness

"Fitness is something that happens to you while you're practicing good technique."

If the swimmers in my camps go home with little else, I want them to go home remembering that. It's the cornerstone of the whole Total Immersion program, and though I may sound repetitious with what I'm about to say, it can hardly be overstressed: 70 percent of your swim speed comes from your stroke mechanics and only 30 percent from the muscles, the heart—all the systems that power that stroke. After the second or third time I repeat it at a camp, I can see an excited idea forming in some of the athletes' eyes. "Wow! This guy tells me I don't have to be trained to be good! What a time-saver!"

Alas, that's not what I meant. We're adjusting priorities, not advocating sloth. In the first place, 30 percent is nothing to walk away from. More importantly, however, even a brilliantly efficient stroke won't do you much good if you run out of gas halfway down the pool. Training does have its place in the Total Immersion system, and the more you know about what the training effect is, the better you'll know how to plan your own.

My definition is simple: The training effect can be summed up as the feeling of nearly limitless capacity to exercise, take deep, satisfying breaths, feel fresh throughout a workout, and go on practically forever. It's really the opposite of aging—asking ourselves (and our cells) to do *more* rather than less. That's why I didn't savor it fully until I'd begun to experience aging first. See if what happened to me sounds familiar.

I was in the best shape of my life during four years of college swimming. Rigorous daily two-hour workouts gave me the ability to tirelessly swim mile after hard mile. I had energy to burn for anything I wanted to do. But you're *supposed* to feel that way when you're 20 years old.

That must have been why I gave it up so casually, retiring from competitive swimming before I'd even turned 21. Masters swimming wasn't an option back then, and without races to train for, what was the point in working out?

Sixteen sedentary years followed. The lean and hard undergraduate's body softened into the daddy-and-breadwinner's flabby frame, easily winded from just raking leaves. I wasn't happy about it, but I'd grown comfortable with my undemanding lifestyle.

Soon after my 37th birthday, the wake-up call came. Reaching into the backseat of my car for a light package, I couldn't straighten up again. Three days later, able to get out of bed for the first time, I promised myself I would return to regular swim training.

Predictably, the first months were difficult and discouraging as I struggled to overcome the accumulated effects of neglect on my muscles, heart, and lungs. A hard, four-mile training session had been a cakewalk in college. Now, I could barely struggle through one mile. But I kept at it, swimming the short, brisk lengths of intervals instead of just plowing up and down in nonstop marathon workouts, until it got easier and I could go farther.

Day by day, week by week, for the next several years, my capacity grew. In year two I could knock off 3,000-yard practices as easily as the 2,000-yard workouts of the year before. By the third, I had deftly upped it to 4,000 yards and in the fourth, as I trained for a 5,000-meter (3.1 miles) event at the World Masters Championships, I could sail through sessions of 5,000 yards and more without even breathing hard. Best of all, as I turned 40, I felt much *younger* than I had 10 years earlier.

So, besides an elixir for turning back the clock, what *is* the training effect? Building strength through stress. Philosopher Friedrich Nietzsche might have been thinking of the benefits we get from our workouts when he declared, "That which does not kill me makes me stronger." Stress an organism and it breaks down a little, then builds itself up slightly better than before. Give a muscle a heavier weight to lift than it's used to and it has to work harder. Ouch. Put it on a *regular program* of such work, however, and it builds itself up so it can meet that new demand easily—as long as it gets enough rest between workouts to repair and strengthen itself. It's a ratcheting process: one step back, rest, two steps forward.

The starting point for training is not the mirror, as some people looking for "good bodies" mistakenly believe, but the heart—a muscle we can develop just like any other. The amount of work your heart can do is called cardiac output—the volume of blood it can circulate in a given period of time. The goal of training is to increase cardiac output, which determines how much work your muscles can do.

Cardiac output is the product of heart rate (pulse, or beats per minute [bpm]) multiplied by stroke volume (the amount of blood it can pump with each beat). Stress the heart regularly through exercise and it will grow bigger and stronger just as other muscles do. This increases stroke volume. As your heart gets better able to pump more blood with each contraction, it takes fewer contractions to do the job. So as your training takes hold, you can either do the same work (like swimming a mile) at the same speed more easily (you *feel* better), or you can work just as hard as you used to but go faster (you *do* better). The same effort that once produced a 40-minute mile may now drive you through the mile in 35 minutes. That's the choice most people make.

The other muscles, of course, also respond to training. They learn how to better extract oxygen from the blood to fuel themselves and flush out waste products, and they may increase their size.

Training (and How to Get It) — — — — — — — — —

The heart gets its training from most any workout. But most of the blood it circulates goes to the skeletal muscles doing the actual work of moving the body around the track or down the pool. Since swimming uses different muscle groups from running, for example, swim-training builds you differently from running. And you can't get around that by just pouring more work on, as I'm reminded every year. If I've spent all winter prepping ambitiously for a springtime Regional or National Masters championship, by April I'll be in prime shape for swimming three miles of brisk interval repeats—the equivalent of 12 running miles. Won't even break a sweat. But on my first spring run about the same time, I'm shot after three easy miles. Plenty of cardiac output; however, the running muscles have lost the ability to use it well. But if I persevere through that discouraging phase, within weeks I'll begin to feel stronger—much more quickly than if my cardiovascular system wasn't already in "swimming shape."

That's the value of cross-training.

That's also a lesson in specificity. For example, don't train your cycling muscles to become a better swimmer. In fact, as I mentioned in an earlier chapter, specificity goes even deeper than just narrowing most of your training to the sport you want to excel at. You even use specialized muscle groups at different times *within* that single sport, such as when you swim different strokes. If I train with freestyle sets, then race breaststroke with all I've got, I can count on my muscles starting to shut down midway through the event. The breaststroke muscles aren't in racing shape. As much swimming as I've done, they haven't been specifically trained.

And finally, even if you train exactly the right muscles every single time, they respond differently to different workout intensities. There's *aerobic* (with oxygen) training, where the muscles burn fuel to produce energy and can go on doing that for a long time. And there's *anaerobic* (without oxygen) training, which is more intense, relies on a kind of stored muscle fuel that doesn't require oxygen but that's always in limited supply, and makes you tired quickly.

Aerobic and anaerobic fitness are not only powered by different energy sources, they are used at different times. The aerobic source provides energy at moderate rates, but for a long time, as we said. This promotes endurance. The anaerobic source provides energy faster, perfect for bursts of speed, but the well goes dry quickly. It's like having two fuel tanks, one with a huge valve and one with a tiny one. The huge valve will power an equally huge eight-cylinder engine —but not for long. The tank empties quickly. The small valve may run only a meager four-cylinder engine but will keep it going all day long.

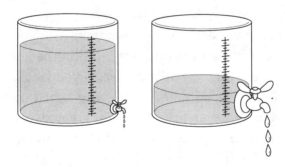

If you like to swim fast, and especially if you race, the training challenge is to make sure the anaerobic fuel tank is topped off. You could swim 10,000 aerobic yards a day and still have little but fumes in that other tank. The only way to fill it is anaerobic training.

Easy to say, not so easy to do. Anaerobic hurts! And the more anaer-

Training (and How to Get It) — — — — — — — — —

obic your training is, the more your lungs burn, your chest pounds, and your muscles throb. That's why it's so easy to put off over and over again. But if you want to race—as opposed to just get in shape—you can't make it purely on aerobic fitness.

The shorter the race, the more anaerobic it will be. In a race of 50 yards, which might take between 30 and 40 seconds, about 90 percent of your energy comes from the anaerobic fuel tank. But in the mile race, which usually takes between 20 and 30 minutes, more than 90 percent of the energy will come from your aerobic tank.

Conveniently, the way you should train for each event is much the same as the way you race it. Endurance training (longer sets, shorter rest, easier pace) develops the "wind" tank. Sprint training (shorter sets, longer rest, faster pace) develops the "speed" tank by making you swim fast enough and hard enough so your muscles scream for more oxygen. If they have to scream often enough, they eventually learn to extract more oxygen from the blood.

That's called higher maximal oxygen uptake (the VO_{2max} of seasoned athlete's lingo), but it's not the only way to skin the aerobic/anaerobic speed cat. The other way is—no surprise to you by now, I'm sure—a better stroke. Since 70 percent of your swim speed comes from your stroke, as I obviously never tire of saying, great stroke mechanics let you reach much higher speeds without doing much more work or using more fuel. Swim economically, minimizing drag with a sleek and balanced body, and you'll automatically be able to go faster before crossing the dreaded *anaerobic threshold.*

Still, what happens if you train one way and race another? Aren't the two really close enough to give decent results? No, they're not. I learned that myself the hard way.

Several years ago, getting ready for the five-kilometer (3.1-mile) race in the Masters World Championships, I logically used long sets on very short rest for my training. After all, a race lasting over an hour would probably draw maybe a percent or two of its energy from the anaerobic system. Why bother training it?

But I was getting antsy to do *something* with all this conditioning. So, long before the big race, I entered a local Masters meet. The 100-yard freestyle was my first event, and I mounted the block confident that since my high-volume/short-rest training sessions had me in the best shape since college, this would be a very good day.

At first, it was. At the start I dove in and swam strongly through the first 50 yards. But as I came off that second turn, something was wrong. I couldn't possibly be tired! Already?

Oh yes I could. By the time I came to the 75-yard turn, my muscles were tying up into knots and I felt as if I were wearing an overcoat instead of my Speedo. My struggle to finish that brief race gave me plenty of reason to reflect on how nice it would have been to have done at least a little speed training. I may have been in fantastic aerobic shape, but the anaerobic tank was long dry.

So What Are You Training For?

You can't make the most of your training time if you don't know why you're training in the first place. Do you want to be fit and healthy? Become smoother in the water? Build a more powerful body? Win races? They're all good reasons for getting into the pool, and they all take different kinds of preparation.

Of course, in my earliest days as a coach, influenced mainly by my own experiences as a swimmer, I knew none of that. No one else knew it either. We had a tried-and-true notion of what training sessions were supposed to accomplish: Grind it out until you became a successful racer. If you could just keep the pressure on until the guy in the next lane broke, you won. So the coach's job was simple. Keep the pressure on, keep making it harder, keep increasing everyone's tolerance for misery.

The longer I worked with swimmers, though, the more I understood how complex the real training puzzle actually is, how desperately muscles need rest to improve since that's when they do their rebuilding, and how training the nervous system to swim more economically is far more useful than beating up the body anyway. Suddenly, training split into a whole range of choices anyone could fit into. You no longer had to be a college jock in your 20s to be considered "in training," and you didn't have to destroy yourself every day to get where you were going. Because you could be working toward any of the following:

Basic Fitness: Is your goal to simply enjoy aerobic fitness, to feel strong and healthy with plenty of energy to get through the day? You can achieve that with regular 30- to 40-minute swim workouts, three or four times a week. Unless you're gearing up for a swimming race, basic low-intensity sets will give you everything you want. And if your swimming is a break from hard training in another sport, you'll get all the muscle-soothing you need from this kind of workout.

Training Fitness: Fill out a race entry form, and whether you know it or not, basic fitness is no longer enough. No matter whether you plan to eventually suit up for a casual Masters meet, tough open-water swim, or first triathlon, your training program needs to become more ambitious. Training fitness is the ability to handle difficult and demanding workouts.

Training fitness is what you have to achieve before actually getting yourself race-ready. You must prepare to prepare, laying the groundwork for your race training, not just plunging into it. Successful training is a gradual series of small adaptations instead of a sudden overload that puts you down for the count. You'll need to slowly "turn up the volume" with longer sets, longer workouts, and probably more frequent training sessions. And you're going to have to turn up the intensity too, with some of that anaerobic work I spoke of earlier in the chapter. The longer the event you're entering—from the minute or so of a creditable 100-yard freestyle to the three-hours-plus of an Olympic-distance triathlon—the more you'll ask of your body getting ready. You don't go overnight from training two hours a week to as much as two hours a day.

Racing Fitness: Races are simply different from workouts. Most of us go all out when we race (after all, it's a *race!*), but we train at a less punishing pace.

Technically, to set the record straight, there is no such thing as "racing fitness" because it's too broad a term to have any meaning. What you need to be fit for is not just a race but a 100-yard freestyle, or 200 breaststroke or 400 individual medley. If you haven't prepared your body for how—and how hard—it will work in the specific event you're entering, it won't be up to the task.

This is an easy rule to forget. Remember my own minute of race infamy? I'd turned myself into one mean aerobic machine over months of prepping for the steady and brisk clip of a one-hour-plus open-water race of 3.1 miles (5,000 meters). But several months before the big one, I dropped into that 100-yard freestyle event which should have taken me about 58 seconds. Instead, the muscle mutiny that struck barely halfway through my ultimate 60-seconds-plus ordeal was a humbling reminder that if your training doesn't at some point duplicate the oxygen demands of your race, your body will simply turn on you. It likes familiarity, not surprises.

If you compete at different distances and can't possibly specialize in all of them, just decide which one means the most to you and focus mainly on that. The rest will have to take care of themselves. Even coaches have no magic solution to this. My best race is the mile, but I can't resist a sprint now and then. So I do enough aerobic training to turn in decent mile times and squeeze in enough anaerobic work so at least my 100s aren't embarrassing.

Winning fitness: "Full tanks" from building racing fitness let you finish your event and go home happy. Putting power and speed on top of that lets you finish your event and go up to the awards stand for your medal. But power and speed are achieved a little differently in swimming than they are in other sports.

That's one reason some coaches call swimming a power-limited activity. Drag increases exponentially as you speed up. Go twice as fast, the water fights you four times as hard. So you need plenty of power if you want to move quickly. But you can't just go to the weight room to build this kind of power because it has to follow the exact pattern of your stroke—and even be at the same speed. Specificity again.

Swimmers must build this with ultrashort, ultrafast repeats so their muscles learn to throw every available fiber into the job. Since high speed equals high resistance, that's what helps the muscles build the power you'll need them to deliver in a race. It's like loading the heaviest plate on the bar in the weight room, only you get to do it in the pool.

"Ultrashort" is no figure of speech either. Sprinters do their all-out power training in lengths as short as 12 yards and seldom go more than 25, though they sometimes pile on even more drag than the water throws at them by using tubes and paddles. Longer-distance competitors build the kind of power they need just by swimming faster than their race pace. The math is not complicated. Let's say you average 1:20 per 100 meters in a 1,500-meter race (equals a 20-minute finishing time). Doing 100-meter repeats in 1:10—or even 50-meter repeats in 0:35—will improve your swimming power for the 1500.

Power, of course, is not speed, as I explained earlier in this book. A powerful swimmer with lackluster efficiency will remain a powerful swimmer stuck in the middle of the pack. Remember Alexander Popov, possibly the world's greatest competitor? He wins races because his stroke stays longer than anyone else's, even at top speed. Hard enough when you're moving slowly, almost impossible as you sprint. A typical stroke rate in the mile is about 70 per minute. In the 100-meter, it can zoom to 110. And since the distance you travel with each stroke (stroke length) falls off rapidly with even small increases in the number you take per minute (stroke rate), it's easy to start spinning your wheels instead of speeding up. So don't think the most forgiving place to launch your racing career is probably something nice and short. (A race of 200 to 500 yards probably offers the best balance between necessary training preparation and a race duration that allows you to do well by practicing the smart-swimming strategies we teach in this book.) Successful sprinters invest a lot of time in patiently teaching their muscles how to move not just fast but long and smooth too. The muscles that learn best win.

No matter where you are on the training pyramid, perhaps putting down your base or already way up at the top and sharpening your power and speed, the inevitable question is, "How much can I do next?" Most athletes without a coach to hold them on course think they know the secret principle of training: "If some is good, more must be better. So I'll do as much as I can, just as soon as I can." And in this comparatively injury-free sport, they may get away with it.

But it's not the path to success. Progression—strengthening your body by gradually asking it to do more—is one of the most important fundamentals of effective training (see "Training Made Simple" page 159). But in swimming, with so much of your success coming from technical improvements instead of physical ones, it needs to be handled a little differently.

Conventional progression goes like this: Since a muscle continues to adapt only so long as it's asked to do more than it's used to, I can do all the biceps curls I want with a 10-pound weight and my muscles will get very good at that. But they won't be able to lift 15 pounds until I push them. Similarly, if you swim a 35-minute mile every day, your physiology becomes perfectly adapted to the energy requirements for that specific speed. Period. To improve in any way, you must raise the training load either by increasing the volume (swimming more than a mile) or training at higher speeds (usually by breaking the mile into shorter, faster pieces) or decreasing the rest interval between repeats.

The smart swimmer needs to know how and when to rein in progression. In the weight room progression might equal progress, but that's not always true in the water. The thrill of being able to constantly swim farther or faster must be tempered by the knowledge that, in most cases, you're probably sacrificing your form to prove that you're progressing. If that's true, you're not. Whatever you're gaining in fitness is being taken away by the cost of a less effective stroke. I can't say it often enough: To swim better than you ever thought you could, follow the method we teach in my camps and in this book. They're based on establishing efficient stroke habits as a foundation, then adding volume or intensity only as fast as you can handle them with no loss of efficiency.

Don't be surprised if it actually takes more patience and persistence than just throwing a few more laps into the mix every workout or two, as you probably used to do. To beef up your mile swim, your challenge is to add only laps or repetitions you can do with the same efficiency (stroke count) as your best laps, usually your first few. One way is to increase a set of 10 repetitions of 100 yards to 15 repetitions, or keep the number of repetitions at 10 but increase each repeat to 150 yards, while holding the same average stroke count. Another technique is to keep the total yardage of your set the same but cut the rest between reps from 30 seconds to 15, without giving up any efficiency.

For shorter-distance swimmers, the numbers are just a little more involved. If you do 50 yards freestyle in 40 seconds and 30 strokes, can you do it in 38 seconds and 30 strokes? Or let's say your count goes up by four strokes when you speed up to 35 seconds. Can you find a way to hold that speed but have it cost you only two additional strokes? You're making bargains with the water, and you want to make sure you always win. Effective trading of strokes for speed is what made Alexander Popov the most dominant swimmer of his time, and Matt Biondi before him.

So the results are clearly worth it.

Training Made Simple

The Basic Facts of Getting Fit for Swimming or Any Other Endurance Sport

1. *Stress*: Not the kind caused by discovering a bounced check or having a run-in with your abrasive boss. In training, stress simply means a workload imposed on the body. Carefully and selectively applied, it elicits a positive response: The body grows stronger. But if the workload is too heavy, the body can't adapt. The result: injury, exhaustion, frustration.

2. *Progressive Overload*: As the body grows stronger in response to training, gains come more slowly. So we need to increase the load, as long as we do it judiciously and systematically. More frequency or

more intensity—or both—stimulate the body to improve. The right training overload for your first month (or even year) of training probably will be too little to build you up more by the time the third month (or year) comes along.

3. *Specificity*: The body adapts to the specific stress imposed. So your training should be as much as possible like the activity you're preparing for in type, distance, and intensity.

4. *Consistency*: Even if you can spare as little as 30 minutes a day for training, you can still achieve reasonably good fitness by being regular about it. Physiologists tell us that we need to train at least three to four days a week, year-round, to maintain basic fitness. (More fitness obviously takes more work.) Fitness can be easily lost in a few idle weeks, and it always takes longer to regain than it did to lose. So, during a period when your training time threatens to dry up altogether, remember that even a little is far better than none at all.

5. *Progression*: The nearer you get to the top of the mountain you're trying to climb, the steeper it grows. The more you improve, the harder it becomes to keep improving at the same rate. You'll reach 90 percent of your potential with a moderate amount of effort, and beyond that even small gains will come grudgingly. When you reach that point, you're smarter to buff, not build. Polish technique. Swim smarter, not harder. The good news: the fitness ground you've already won will be relatively easy to hold.

6. *Recovery*: Work and rest are yin and yang, inseparable halves of the same equation. You need to recuperate from hard training, to *allow* your body to adapt and successfully handle harder workloads—during a set, a workout, or a training cycle. You can't push your heart rate near its maximum in a set time and again unless it recovers nearly back to its resting level between efforts. Similarly, intense workouts must be balanced with recovery workouts.

And Now for Something Completely Different
(Strokes, That Is. The Other Three, and the Good They Can Do You)

It may surprise mileage-based athletes like cyclists and runners, but swimmers can be as obsessed with distance as anybody else. And the obsession is just as bad for them.

"But I have forty-five minutes to work out, period," time-pressed athletes grumble when I warn them they'd be better off if they left their comfortable workout ruts and started using more variety. "If I try to fit in all that other stuff, I won't be able to rack up the yardage I need to stay in shape."

But they can, and their bodies know it—only their brains still need convincing. Most people can train two to three times as many muscles in the pool as they do now, in whatever time they have to spend, and get just as much conditioning from their workout.

In 45 minutes, a determined swimmer can cover 2,000 to 2,500 yards of freestyle. Since it's the fastest and easiest stroke, it gives the most satisfying total. Mixing in other strokes could chop that comforting number by several hundred yards, and swimmers believe as much as anyone else in the magical power of distance to measure a "good" physical workout. Farther equals fitter.

Except that the muscle you're targeting the most doesn't know that: The heart doesn't understand or care what strokes you're

continued

swimming or how many yards you write in your log. It knows only two things—how hard it has worked and for how long. So let's compare the heart-health effect of two different 20-minute workout sets.

Set #1: 1,000 yards freestyle (10 repeats of 100 yards), leaving every two minutes. John, a 56-year-old Masters swimmer, averages 1:35 for each repeat of the set and keeps his heart rate around 120.

Set #2: Later John decides to swim a 20-minute individual medley set (all four strokes), but now he can complete only eight repeats of 100 yards in the same time since he has to increase his interval to two minutes 30 seconds per 100 yards (two minutes swimming, 30 seconds rest). Once again his heart rate stays around 120 bpm.

What did he lose by dropping 20 percent of his yardage on the second set? No fitness, certainly. His heart pumped about 2,400 times in #1 and #2. It didn't care how far the body it was servicing traveled. And that would be especially true of the lower-intensity workout levels (60 to 75 percent of MHR [maximum heart rate]) fitness swimmers and cross-trainers stay on.

Better yet, you can actually get in better shape even as your yardage goes down. The secret is simple: variety. The heart may not care whether you're swimming one stroke or another, but your muscles care very much. Different muscle groups do the work in each of the four swimming strokes—freestyle, butterfly, breast, and back—because the strokes themselves are so different. A freestyle set helps your freestyle muscles but neglects others. Want to work the greatest amount of muscle tissue? Swim all the strokes. You'll be getting the classic double-barreled benefit of cross-training: better conditioning, with less chance of injury.

7. *Cycles:* Steady, "submaximal" training is like putting money in the bank, establishing our base, our security. We write checks on that account with the demands of intensive training. Write too many and you'll soon be bankrupt, your body will rebel and simply refuse to adapt (see page 159). And the faster and harder you train, the sooner you'll get your body's "insufficient funds" notice. This applies to individual workouts as well as training cycles of months and years. Adult swimmers especially should remember: Your "careers" may be measured in quarter- or even half-centuries, enviable to be sure. If you mainly want health and happiness, steady low-stress training will keep you injury-free, physically fresh, and fit for the long haul, week-in and week-out, year-in and year-out.

Chapter 10

No-Sweat Swimming

(Why Going Slow Will Get You There Faster)

Let's slow down for just a minute. Despite all our talk in the last chapter about fast training, speed isn't everything when it comes to swimming well. There are times, in fact, when it's not even a very good idea and can actually do you more harm than good. The way I teach swimming, you can't become really proficient without a fair amount of slow—I prefer to call it *effective*—swimming.

Does that get your attention? It should. It's not only good news, it happens to be correct despite the fact that, as I said in the last chapter, you sometimes need to get yourself good and winded to fill up your anaerobic fuel tank if you expect to be able to take it to the limit in a race. Also, as we'll see in the next chapter, you must be willing to swim with one eye on the clock and the other on the lane lines. But in the Total Immersion system, nothing does as much for your stroke as careful, thoughtful practice at a pace that lets you stroke effectively and move efficiently. Learn to do that and speed will come more easily anyway.

That's not a popular notion in the athletic profession, and you'll have no trouble finding swim coaches who disagree with me. Too bad there's such an abundance of people convinced you must train hard all the time to improve at swimming, people who have helped establish popular training gospel. When top swimmers get written up, their prowess is inevitably credited to a litany of extraordinary sacrifices and ferocious work habits.

But coaches don't know it all. In fact, there's more and more they can learn from the work of the swim community's scientists.

And one of the things they're gradually learning—though they're fighting it tooth and nail—is that easy swimming is a formidably effective training tool, even for top racers.

Take Alexander Popov—again. You don't get to be indisputably the best in the world without knowing a thing or two about technique and how to get it. So what can we make of the fact that even though Popov's best events are the shortest, fastest, most anaerobic in all of swimming, nearly 70 percent of his workout yardage for the entire year preceding the last Olympics was below the so-called anaerobic threshold? If you said it must be because Popov knew it did him more good, you were right. He was breathing comfortably, patiently laying down tracks in his nervous system for an ultraefficient stroke that would later stand firm and propel him effectively during the precisely administered hard, fast work he would also do.

Coaches can't cling to the "no pain, no gain" defense anymore either. While they have always followed the gospel that more and harder are better, the physiologists have at least gotten them to admit that adding in some *easier* produces superior results. Until recently, in swimming especially, the recovery period was the best-kept secret in training. Recovery, you'll remember from the last chapter, is when the adaptations you want—like your muscles growing stronger—actually take place. Too bad that for so many years most coaches, believing the only good time was work time, were reluctant to take a chance by taking it easy on their swimmers at regular intervals. Training policy was like the proverbial line in the sand: Can't stand the heat? Get out of the pool. Philosopher Nietzsche, coaches agreed, knew how to shape a swimmer: "That which doesn't kill you makes you stronger."

Unless it makes you exhausted and weaker. Too much hard work results in what scientists call failing adaptation syndrome. The body, seeing no glimmer of light at the end of the hard/harder/hardest tunnel, gives up on ever getting a chance to adapt and just slowly collapses. Athletes grow tired, slow, and weak . . . if they don't get sick or injured first. Some swim coaches accept this decline with their eyes open, counting on a precompetition taper to pull everything out of the fire. Beat 'em up bad, then rest the dickens out of them, and your swimmers will come through big time, eh, Big Guy?

And so they might. Their bodies are so grateful for finally getting a chance to catch their breaths (figuratively and literally) that they "superadapt," as the scientists say, taking a big leap forward. Unfortunately, the coaches then give all the credit to the hard work, even though it may have actually pushed the swimmers perilously close to coming apart. And as traditional coaches, they'd never admit it was the rest that finally allowed the athletes to reach their true potential.

But the scientists have been talking a little louder lately, and they've begun to get through. "Uh, Coach, wouldn't it make more sense to build your athletes up in a series of small steps? Work a little, rest a little, then work a little harder? Kind of ratchet them up from each level to the new one?" Makes more sense than drowning everybody in training, triggering a long stale period, then turning them loose with one big miraculous recovery at the end.

"And oh, yes, your swimmers might enjoy it more."

So coaches have grudgingly begun to accept the wisdom of training their athletes more scientifically, permitting more easy days, maybe even—*subversive thought!*—a whole week now and then of relaxed and low-key training. They grumble, mind you, over violating their dearest training commandment. Some even disdainfully call it garbage yardage. Most swimmers like it (others, the bedrock traditionalists, would still rather have Nietzsche running workouts), but many aren't benefiting as much as they could because the coaches still see a day of easy swimming as a regrettably necessary "backing off." They don't understand it's a major opportunity.

But champion Alexander Popov's coach understood this long ago.

No-Sweat Swimming (Why Going Slow Will Get You There Faster) — —

It's not just recovery, he knew, it's a way to allow aerobic adaptations you've already earned—your very conditioning—to finally happen. It's also the only good way to train your nervous system to use that conditioning in the most efficient possible way. When your heart's humming along at 130 or 140 bpm, you can work on precise skills and techniques that are impossible when it's pounding at 180. Things like stroke drills, sensory swimming, stroke-limited swims, and speed without "stroke cost." And since your body's ability to swim with maximum efficiency is far more critical than its ability to swim with maximum effort, it's clear the time spent on easy laps is probably not just as important but *more* important.

And Popov will prove to be just the tip of the iceberg when the easy-training news finally gets around. In the mid-1990s, Russian swimmers held every freestyle world record from the 50 through the 400 meters. Inevitably, the coaches of America's elite athletes will start to get the idea too.

But cutting-edge training usually takes much longer to filter down to the self-coached adult. And if any one group of athletes needs the advice more than any other, it's triathletes. Just think: *Three* sports to push yourself to exhaustion in! Plus the fanciful cross-training notion that hard work in one sport somehow qualifies as recovery from hard work in another. So they hammer in running, hammer in biking, and hammer in swimming, then wonder why they spend half their lives nursing injuries.

Grinding out run and bike miles may do some good, since those less technical sports get a bigger boost from gains in basic physical prowess. But hard swim-training makes no sense at all for the average triathlete whose best bet is to never, never, never swim hard. Figure it out. In the race itself, victory always goes to the fastest biker or runner, never (never, never) to the fastest swimmer. There's even a word for triathletes who work hard during the swim leg. They're called losers. These earnest types struggle to a small lead out of the water while everybody else sits back and comfortably drafts behind them, getting pulled along. The strugglers quickly get swallowed up on the bike and finally collapse altogether on the run. Everyone who coasted through the swim goes on to ride and run to glory.

So for the multisport among you, the bottom line is this: Since your smartest move in a triathlon is to keep your heart rate at 130 to 140 for the entire swim, training at anything higher is a waste of time and energy. Your take-it-easy work will pay big dividends if only you follow these two points:

1. Remember our familiar rule of 70 (performance is determined 70 percent by stroke efficiency and only 30 percent by fitness), and take advantage of it against your competition. Only a tiny fraction of triathletes come from a competitive-swimming background. Most are former runners, who are generally very fit but who also have just rudimentary swimming skills. There's your chance, and it's a huge opportunity. Instead of working out, *practice,* using the Total Immersion methods I've covered in this book.

2. Remember too that swimming is the best way to speed up your recovery from hard work in other sports like biking and running. Dial down the swimming effort, concentrate on fine-tuning your nervous-system training instead of wasting work on your already superb aerobic machinery, and you'll bounce back fitter and faster. That in turn will make you a stronger runner and cyclist, since those sports no longer have to share scarce aerobic-adaptation resources with swimming. This is not wishful thinking or clever wordplay. Triathletes have told me over and over that it happens to them once they adjust their training to the Total Immersion method. Did I give them secret tips

about running or biking? Of course not. I'm a swim coach. But I could help them in those other sports nonetheless by making them smarter swim-trainers.

And what about that other competitive group, Masters swimmers (technically anyone over 19, but in practice mostly swimmers from 30 to 90-plus)? They too know that better swim times come from punching up their aerobic powers. Only one problem with that. Most are 40 and over, and they've had plenty of time to work on their cardiovascular conditioning. And with nature beginning to lower the ceiling just a little anyway, pushing cardiovascular conditioning any higher—unless you've just been sitting around for a long time—is unlikely. So any future personal bests will come from better stroke mechanics, not from scaling some new training heights.

What if you couldn't care less about racing in the first place? Does it really make any difference whether you try to blast from one end of the pool to the other or plan careful, measured practices? Indeed it does. And there are literally millions of people who need to know that. Considering that there are maybe 50,000 racers and somewhere between 4 and 5 million fitness swimmers, about 99.9 percent of all swimmers have less interest in whether they're swimming fast or slow than in whether they're staying healthy and strong and having fun along the way. They need to know they can get 100 percent of the benefits and enjoyment they seek without ever breaking a sweat.

Why, even racers generally know that most of the changes in your body that transform you into an athlete occur at heart rates well below the so-called anaerobic threshold, the point where you get seriously out of breath. Your cardiac output improves more efficiently, you burn more fat, and you build more basic endurance at lower heart rates. And if that sounds like a complete list of the most important antiaging effects, that's because it is. Your muscles get stronger in the bargain.

So what's missing? Just the anaerobic training you need for racing. But if you're not going to race anyway, who needs it? You can still steadily improve because your easy aerobic training will let you maximize your efficiency more and more and more. You're less likely to suffer injuries or staleness and more apt to train consistently since you don't need the periods of rest and recovery demanded by hard training, and you'll find it's easier to make swimming match the schedules of your everyday life.

For all but the elite among us, I say haste makes waste. Speed up your swimming improvement by slowing down your training.

Chapter 11

Time to Get Organized—Swimming by the Clock

Are you a pool robot? Pool robots are swimmers who just jump in and start swimming, like a big toy with fresh batteries, plodding mechanically up and down and up and down. It's the work ethic with a dash of chlorine. And even though training like this is the least effective, it's how too many of us willingly squander our training time. That's why we're about to discuss intervals—a much better way to work out.

Meantime, if the description above sounds like you, don't be embarrassed. You have plenty of company. You may also be smiling broadly because it seems to you like that last chapter on slow swimming finally justified your mind-numbing, metronomic workouts. In fact, it did no such thing. Yes, you need a certain amount of purposeful, thoughtful swimming to build skills, but end-less workouts with no objective are dead-end exercise.

In the Total Immersion program we want to be sure you don't put speed before good technique, so we don't stress a lot of timed swimming early on. But staying in second gear is not the point either. To get ahead, you need a plan, you need structure, and you probably need some workouts where you push the throttle a bit harder.

You need intervals. And in this chapter, you shall have them. But not the scary, swim-'til-you-drop exercises in exhaustion most people think of when they hear the word. Total Immersion intervals are scientific swimming that make the most of your time without asking you to beat yourself up.

Although many of us probably know that hanging out on medium-throttle autopilot until our energy or time runs out won't take us far, it's how most fitness swimmers spend their time. Grab them between laps—if you can get them to stop at all—and you'll hear why: "I want to swim a mile." Like the 10K in running, it's a kind of gold-standard distance against which everyone wants to measure him- or herself.

Nobody understands this better than pool lifeguards, who know from experience that nearly every new swimmer will come up at one time or other asking, "How many laps to the mile here?" Most pools now simply post the number for all to see. Armed with that intelligence (in a 25-yard pool, by the way, the magic figure is 70.4), they begin trying to chip away at the mountain. If they can't make it nonstop right away, they'll settle for doing it piecemeal. Knock off three sets of 20, then finish up with an easy 10 or 12. The goal is inevitably to go longer and rest less until they can finally patch it all together into one nonstop triumph. They congratulate themselves, as well they might, but the glow doesn't last long. Because tomorrow, naturally, they've got to come back and swim it *faster.* Then that new challenge remains interesting for awhile until the times simply level off and go nowhere. All that's apparently left then is to soldier on because "it's good for you."

That's not you? For one thing, you don't have the time to squander on that kind of distance? Well, then, maybe you're the clock-watching type who dashes into the health club at lunchtime with 40 minutes to spare. On day one, you probably peter out after 10 or 20 lengths (to coaches and competitive swimmers, by the way, a length and a lap are the same), even with a minute or two of rest between each. But you keep whittling away just as any would-be miler would, adding laps, subtracting rest, anxious to pump up that 40-minute lap score. And true enough, after awhile you'll probably be able to swim the full 40 minutes without stopping, which may even add up to a mile (70 lengths). With luck, you'll even be able to pile on a couple more lengths just for good measure. But eventually you too will reach your swimming equilibrium ("terminal mediocrity," one of my campers called it) and the end of anything remotely interesting about your workouts.

That's what always comes of making the lap tally the holy grail of your swimming. You waste time fretting over how many or how fast —instead of how *right*—you are doing each one. Instead, you should be fretting about stagnation. The body gets so used to what you're doing that there's no stimulus to improve. The principles of adaptation and overload will see you through for awhile in the beginning since, if you've never swum a mile, the preparation for it is an overload which does train your body. But once you've done the mile and done it again, where do you go? The world's best swimmers, the human fish who train with coaches, are always baffled by the lap swimmer's dead-end routine. "Doesn't it get boring?" they ask, since they know there's a much better way to invest their time. "Well, yes," answers the lap swimmer. "But it's good for me."

Well it could be a lot better for you and a lot more fun too if you'd switch to intervals or, for the less technical, to what I call stopping-on-purpose-with-a-plan. You need to know how to make the clock work for you. So let's do some interval training the Total Immersion way.

Why Is That Clock Missing a Hand?

The pace clock, that big, octagonal, white-faced moon with the sweep hand on the wall near the end of virtually every lap pool in America, is the key to your graduation from pointless swimming to smart interval training. Since swimmers measure performance in minutes and seconds, the pace clock has a minute hand and a sweep hand, but no hour hand. One minute—one sweep of the second hand around the clock face—is divided into 12 five-second intervals. The five-second intervals (:05–:10, :10–:15, etc.) are shown with both a red mark and large black numbers. The four marks (seconds) between them are black marks. Swimmers usually start their repeats on a red (five-second) mark.

The pace clock tells you everything you need to know for effective interval training, whether you're coached or uncoached. Read it to find out 1.) how fast you've swum each repeat, and 2.) how much rest remains before your next one.

Use it as a tool, not a tyrant. Become too absorbed with the pace clock and you'll allow it to grow into an unforgiving taskmaster. Swimmers who meticulously focus only on how fast they're swimming and never mind the efficiency price (how many strokes, how high a heart rate) are really practicing sloppy swimming. But use the clock as a valuable tool to help build up your technique, and it will make all your practices more valuable. And more fun.

Total Immersion intervals are a little different from what you may be used to. Most athletes use the "i" word to broadly describe any training that's tough, repetitive, leaves you out of breath, and gets you ready for a race. Work out, throw up, go home.

I use them differently. Yes, there are intervals that can prepare you for an all-out race. But there are dozens of others as well. The questions I get most often, and the answers you need to train the Total Immersion way, are:

1. *What Effect Can I Expect?* In Total Immersion swimming, the objective of anything we do—intervals included—is improvement of technique, whether you're learning new skills, consolidating them through practice, or testing how well you can hold onto them as you swim farther and faster.

Building endurance, increasing speed, improving your tolerance for anaerobic training, and practicing racing or pacing strategies are worthwhile secondary objectives which you should expect from your intervals. But they are *secondary.*

2. *How Many Should I Do?* Decide this way: Do enough to give yourself adequate aerobic conditioning (a set lasting at least 10 to 15 minutes —including swim and rest time—in a workout of four or five sets). But don't do so many that your technique or concentration suffers.

3. *How Far Should I Go?* Repeats can technically be any distance from 25 yards to 800 yards or more, but for stroke improvement, which is the name of our game, shorter ones are nearly always better. While longer repeats help develop endurance and pace sense, they generally undermine speed and technique. Shorter repeats (generally 200 yards and less) don't have this disadvantage and can give you virtually everything you want. For greater endurance, increase the number of repeats and/or decrease the rest. For more speed, choose fewer, faster repeats and more rest.

4. *Must I Swim All-Out?* No indeed. First of all, you can measure intensity in several ways: percent of maximum heart rate, percent of maximum speed, or perceived exertion (how hard does it *feel?*). Higher intensity develops more speed and anaerobic fitness. Lower intensity is better for development of technique, for improving aerobic fitness, and for practice of pacing: learning to swim at the same speed for a long time, even as you grow more tired.

5. *How Much Rest Is Enough?* Your fitness (aerobic endurance) goes up fastest when the rest period between swims is one-half or less of the swim time, usually shown as a work:rest ratio of 2:1. Ratios of 3:1 all the way up to 10:1 are common in building endurance, and you'll see them often in swim-training books. When you do, watch out. In Total Immersion, technique and efficiency come before absolutely everything else, so be careful that your intervals are challenging

enough to promote fitness, yet not so tight you have to throw away efficiency as you fight fatigue to do them.

Work:rest ratios of 1:1, 1:2, etc. (equal or more rest than work), develop speed and anaerobic fitness since the longer rest lets you swim them much faster. A short rest interval doesn't allow enough recovery for an all-out push.

6. Are All Repeats Straight Swimming? Not at all. The variety is limitless. You can drill, drill-swim, or just swim. Use any of the four strokes you want to practice. Work on pulling and kicking with or without a pull buoy and/or kickboard. (More on use of these and other training tools in Chapter 13). Even make every interval different from the one before—descending sets, pyramids, ladders, etc. (More on this below.)

Basic Intervals: Four Good Ways to Watch the Clock

1. Fixed-rest Sets

> Example: 4 x 200 yards on 60 seconds rest
> Number of repetitions: 4
> Distance of each rep: 200 yards
> Start each repetition: 60 seconds after finishing the last one

You don't get intervals more basic than this, so it's the place to start if you're new. You're guaranteed the same amount of rest, no matter how slowly or how fast you swim. For instance, do the first 200 in 3:00 and you start the second at the 4:00 mark. If your second 200 slows to 3:20, you start the third at 4:20, holding your minute's rest no matter what.

To make it easier to keep track, most swimmers round off the rest to leave on a red mark on the clock. After a 200 at 3:17, they'd probably go again at 4:15 or 4:20, not 4:17.

2. Fixed-interval Sets

Example: 8 x 100 yards on 2:00
Number of repetitions: 8
Distance of each rep: 100 yards
Start each repetition on: 2:00 (includes swim time plus rest time)

This is fairly basic too, but it's a little tougher and more strategic than #1. You start each 100-yard repeat two minutes after starting the previous one, regardless of how much or little rest that gives you. Finish the first 100 in 1:30 and you get :30 off. Slip to a 1:35 pace on the second and your rest before you start your third repeat slips too: to :25. The only way to keep the slope from getting steeper and steeper—and each repeat from probably getting harder and harder— is to keep up, which means swimming close to the same pace on all eight. Since your tank gets lower each time, you have to figure how to parcel out the work (we explain this in our next chapter on racing) a little better each time so you end up swimming numbers one and eight at the same speed.

3. Decreasing-interval Sets

Example: 5 x 50 yards on intervals of 1:00-:55-:50:45
Number of repetitions: 4
Distance of each rep: 50 yards
Start each repetition on: decreasing rest (see page 180)

Decreasing-interval sets are tougher yet than #2 because on each successive repeat, as you're growing more tired, you automatically get less rest.

Take the example above. The first interval (preceding the second repeat) is 1:00, the next is :55, and the last is :45. So if you swam each repeat in :40, you'd rest :20 before swimming the second, :15 before starting the third, :10 before the fourth, and just :05 before the fifth.

Not for sissies. But believe it or not, an accomplished repeat swimmer can actually swim slightly faster on each succeeding repeat, regaining a sliver of lost rest.

Decreasing intervals are often used by coaches to get you used to the tough challenge of holding your pace in a race, when everything in your body is beginning to say, "Hey, take it easy, will you?"

4. Increasing-interval Sets

> Example: 8 x 50 (1–4 on 1:00, 5–8 on 1:30)
> Number of repetitions: 8
> Distance of each rep: 50 yards
> Start each repetition on: 1:00 for first half, 1:30 for second

This seems like it gives you a break, since you get :30 more rest before each repetition in the second half than in the first. But there's a catch: With that extra rest, you're supposed to swim faster. (And if you do, as we now know, you get still more rest if you're swimming fixed intervals like these.)

The increasing interval is usually used by coaches to speed you up as the set progresses, since the added rest makes the intervals easier to swim harder and faster. It's a kind of rehearsal for finishing a set (and hopefully a race) strongly.

Interval design is limited only by a coach's creativity, and over the years many of us have gotten pretty creative. In fact, you could probably write a whole book just on the elaborate schemes that have been devised to organize your pool time with your eye on the pace clock.

"Descending sets" are sets that grow faster one by one, "ladders" and "pyramids" either increase the length of each rep, or increase it for half the set and then shorten it again on the other half. If that's not enough to keep track of, rest changes too since it's usually calculated from the length of the leg you've just done. And in mixed-distance sets everything is in play, with distances and rest intervals changing and changing again.

But the four bread-and-butter interval formats above will give you the most direct route to improvement, and they don't take a water-proof calculator to keep track of. Besides, it's what you put into each length—not how elaborately your whole program is organized—that gets results.

The "starter kit" below uses nothing fancier than fixed-rest sets. But it will groom you for any goal from basic fitness to a race time you'll be proud of. Just make sure you follow the weekly yardage guidelines. The tougher work, for race-readiness and speed, is like a powerful medicine. You should take just the prescribed amount for best results. More is not better—and can be harmful.

Ready, Set, Repeat!

1. Fitness Intervals

   (60% to 100% of total training yardage)

This is relatively slow, easy swimming that builds aerobic endur-ance. The aim is *extensive* rather than *intensive* training. Speed (or heart rate) is only 65 to 75 percent of your maximum for the repeat distance (i.e., if your best time for 100 yds was 1:20, you would repeat at 1:45 to 2:00 in a fitness interval set). Besides, speed is also held down by short rest periods. To work, the set should be at least 20 minutes. If you're prepping for an extremely long event (e.g., an Iron-man distance swim), it can be made as long as an hour by adding more repeats.

Examples:
16–30 x 50 (10–20 seconds rest)
10–20 x 75 (10–20 seconds rest)
8–15 x 100 (10–30 seconds rest)
5–10 x 150 (15–30 seconds rest)
4–8 x 200 (15–40 seconds rest)

Remember the bedrock principle of the Total Immersion program? "Fitness is something that happens to you while you're practicing good technique." Fitness intervals are a perfect example. You can build fitness *and* efficiency at the same time simply by turning your fitness intervals into drills, drill-swims, sensory skill practice, or other skill-building technique. Try some of these typical combinations:

1. **Drill:** 16 x 50 slide & glide (or your choice) on 20 seconds rest
2. **Drill-swim:** 12 x 75 on 20 seconds rest (50 drill—25 swim)
3. **Sensory skill practice:** 8 x 100 on 20 seconds rest (50 swim downhill—50 swim with a weightless arm)
4. **Stroke eliminators:** 8 x 100 on 20 seconds rest (hold at 17–18 strokes per length [s/l], assuming a "normal" s/l (strokes per length) of 19–20)
5. **Swimming golf:** 8 x 50 on 20 seconds rest. Add strokes and time for each repeat to get score for each repeat, and try to reduce your score between reps one and eight.

2. Race Readiness Intervals

(0% to 30% of total training yardage)

The best way to get ready for a race is to race, so on these intervals you simulate the speeds and physical stresses you'll face after the gun goes off. The usual goal is to make your cardiovascular system and skeletal muscles more able to tolerate oxygen debt. (Muscles need more than the CV system can deliver.) The Total Immersion goal goes a step further: to let you practice holding onto your efficiency at racing speeds. You do that by trying to minimize the difference in s/l between your fitness intervals and your speed intervals. Your total should not increase by more than 10 percent on speed intervals, so if you hold 18 on fitness intervals, don't take more than 20 on speed intervals.

A work:rest ratio of 1:1 should provide enough recovery to let you reach 80 percent or more of maximum speed (and heart rate) on each repeat, which is where you should do your race readiness intervals.

Examples:
(Total distance of repeats should equal 60 to 100 percent of race distance. Example: to prep for 1,500 meters, do sets of 20–30 x 50, or 10–15 x 100.)
8–30 x 50 (30–60 seconds rest)
6–20 x 75 (45–90 seconds rest)
4–15 x 100 (60 seconds—2 minutes rest)
(Count strokes or play swimming golf on all.)

3. Speed intervals

(0% to 10% of total training yardage)

These are your racing "finishing school," since they work on every-thing you need in a race—the anaerobic system, swimming-specific power, and your ability to stay efficient at race speeds—by letting you swim distances shorter than the race at race pace or faster. Your Total Immersion goal is to produce the most speed on the lowest possible stroke count. The work:rest ratio is 1:2 to 1:3. Sets and repeats are short and are only done once or, at most, twice a week.

Examples:
8 x 25 (40–60 seconds rest) for 50–100 yard races
4–10 x 50 (90 seconds to 3 minutes rest) for 100–200 yard races
4–8 x 75 (2–3 minutes rest) for 100–200 yard races
3–8 x 100 (3–5 minutes rest) for 500–1,650 yard races
(Count strokes or play swimming golf on all.)

Swimming with the pace clock doesn't mean swimming 'til you drop. It does mean swimming smart. Anyone can dive in and just churn up and down the pool until the gas runs out. Many do, thinking speed will make them better athletes regardless of how they get it. But the price they pay in wasted time and lost efficiency is high. Intervals give you a goal instead, and a structured and purposeful way of measuring your progress along the path toward it.

And Total Immersion intervals give you the most direct path of all.

Chapter 12

Racing. It's Just Training With a Twist

The beloved running philosopher and cardiologist Dr. George Sheehan was once asked the difference between a jogger and a runner. His reply was a model of medical brevity: "A race entry form."

A trifle elitist, to be sure, but a clever and necessary distinction in a sport that has its own class system and a vocabulary to match. We don't. In the pool, everyone is a swimmer, period.

But that's not to say swimmers who race aren't a little different from those of us who just do our workouts week-in, week-out. There's something about putting your training on the line, side by side with your peers and in full view of the timers, that focuses you as nothing else can. I recommend it. And with the hundreds of all-comers Masters meets held around the country at practically any time of year, you don't have to be an especially accomplished athlete to feel good about your results when you're done.

If you've already got a meet or two behind you, you know what I mean. If you haven't—or if you'd like to do your next one better armed with a little Total Immersion strategy—please read on.

Lifelong swimmers, by the way, probably have a racing advantage over lifelong competitors in practically any other aerobic sport: Many can actually do better as adults than they did on their high school or college teams. The triumph of middle age over youth? Not at all. Nobody is suggesting that swimming repeals the laws of aging. What we are saying— again—is that so much more of your success comes from good technique instead of sheer fitness, and the Total Immersion program gives you the tools to keep improving your technique—and your times—for many years. So whether you've never raced before or are aiming to topple the personal bests of your youth, the odds of continued improvement are very high.

Don't race for medals. Not at the beginning, at least. Do race because simply entering a competition well in advance creates an anticipation which inevitably give purpose and focus to all your training. And do race because an event swum well, an event you've given your best, is more deeply satisfying than any practice. And do race, above all else, because it's the ultimate test of how well you *have* practiced.

And as we said in Chapter 9, there's no such thing as "generic" race training. You target your event, and you ready yourself specifically for it. Lots of endurance work will make you the world's worst sprinter, and vice versa. Just as in road running, you'll find event lengths to suit any personality—short and sharp speed contests to long tests of endurance and staying power. And the training mix for each is a little different. So pick your "size" (short, medium, or long), read on to find out what you need to do to prep for it, and get started.

Races? There's Small, Medium, and Large

1. Sprints: 50–100 Yards/Meters

When once asked what wins sprint races, world-record-holder and Olympic champion Matt Biondi replied, "Four things: technique, technique, technique, and speed." It doesn't take much endurance to swim as fast as you can for 20 to 90 seconds. A deadly efficient stroke is what you need. Just make sure you can hold your stroke length when you're going as fast as you possibly can, when your heart rate is crashing through the roof and lactic acid is flooding into your hapless and hurting muscles.

Efficiency is so critical in short races because you're probably going 20 to 25 percent faster in the 100 meters than the 1500, for example, and the difference in drag and the power needed to overcome it is enormous. Small inefficiencies become hugely magnified in a sprint.

But you can't overlook the need to supply enough energy and oxygen to muscles that are gulping it down for all they're worth, powering your body through this over-the-top effort. Your system also has to whisk away all that energy-sapping lactic acid as fast as your muscles produce it if they're to keep going.

All that means anaerobic training, of course, and you can't let your stroke get sloppy while pushing the practice pace.

Finally, you need the power that comes from training your neuromuscular system to fire up all available muscle motor units to overcome whatever drag your stroke efficiency hasn't eliminated. That means swimming "power sets," short reps at top effort. (See the appendix for some suggestions.)

2. Middle Distance: 200–400 Yards/Meters

Sometimes called speed/endurance events because they take both, these are among the most difficult to train for. You don't get a break. Speeds are fairly close to the sprint, but you've got to hold on for up to 10 times as long. It's not the higher stroke rate of the shorter sprints that will crack your technique and efficiency but the surprising amount of anaerobic work in these races, even though they're longer and slower than sprints. It's hard to stay fussy about your stroke over an entire quarter-mile without enough air.

Of course, as your technique starts to come apart, the "energy cost" of holding your speed inflates even as you have less and less left with every tick of the stopwatch. So middle-distance racers need a two-pronged training strategy:

1. Long, aerobic sets for endurance—sets that will do far more good if they train the nervous system right along with the aerobic system, focusing on stroke efficiency too

2. Race-pace swimming, to develop endurance at higher speeds and get you used to the stroke rate and anaerobic conditions that make these distances such a thorough test

What it all comes down to is finding and holding the right pace—staying out of oxygen debt, operating aerobically for as long as you can. (The more efficient your stroke, remember, the longer you can hold onto that aerobic state of grace.) It's a hard trick to pull off unless you swim most of the race at an even pace. A blazing first half usually guarantees a painful second half. That's why the world's best middle-distance swimmers almost always swim the second half as fast as or even faster than the first. And mastering that tactic takes practice. (See the appendix for some suggestions.)

3. Distance Swimming: 800 Meters and Up

For the thousands of runners who turn to swimming every year to find less body-punishing workouts and who think of a two-mile footrace as barely the far side of a sprint, the comparatively short distance-horizon in swimming comes as a surprise. The 1,500 meter, which may take a top contender 15 to 20 minutes—nearly the same time as a 5K run—is the longest event most swimmers ever enter. And the marathon's time span of three to five hours, a fairly common experience for runners, is all but unheard of in swimming.

So why all the emphasis on high-yardage training? Because swim coaches believe we must not only develop endurance but "feel for the water," which is really just another way of saying natural efficiency. And they believe it takes years of practice and millions of yards of repetition to develop this.

It doesn't. If you can accelerate the development of an efficient stroke, which is just what you're learning to do in this book, then you can drastically reduce the yardage it takes to prep for an endurance swim. Instead, you work on developing what I call efficiency endurance, the ability to keep your stroke the same whatever distance you swim. Training sets up to half again the distance of your race will do this if you use them to practice and improve your ability to keep your stroke long and efficient, lap after lap after lap.

The second reason coaches push so much high-yardage training on swimmers is to develop the "clock in the head," the instinct for swimming at just the right pace so they don't kill the race by overswimming at the beginning. Distance swimmers practice pacing endlessly, learning how to keep going at the same pace for lap after lap even as fatigue mounts. One way to shorten the learning curve is by swimming descending reps, which we mentioned in the last chapter, in which each one gets progressively faster during a long set. (See the appendix for samples.)

How to Be Ready. Really Ready

Good training doesn't necessarily guarantee a good race. The lead spots go to those who've done their homework, from deciding how much warmup they'll need to knowing how the event plays out, what to expect on every length.

If you've done the homework for a 1,650-yard freestyle (the equivalent of the 1,500-meter event) you can get yourself ready for most anything. Otherwise known as swimming's metric mile, it's 66 lengths of a 25-yard pool, and though it's my personal favorite, I always approach it with a love-hate attitude. Love because it's my best distance and the one in which I've always reached my highest national rankings (a couple of seconds). Hate because it promises lots of pain.

Racing. It's Just Training With a Twist —   —   —   —   —   —   —

I've swum longer races that felt easier. I've *run* longer races more comfortably, even though I'm a much better swimmer than runner. A 45- to 50-minute 10K footrace doesn't seem anywhere near as long as a 1650 in the pool, which I can knock off in maybe 18 or 19 minutes. Even a 5K open-water swim, which took me 68 minutes, was easier than any 1,650-yard race I've ever swum in a pool.

Perhaps it's because of the need for such fierce concentration on keeping your stroke efficient, with every lap feeling harder than the last. Perhaps it's all the flip turns that make it hard to stay aerobic as the laps mount. But whatever the reason, this race tests it all: your mental focus, the staying power of your efficiency, and the quality of your conditioning. So getting ready for it is a virtual punch list for all prerace preparation. Based on personal experience, here's how I advise leading up to and handling a 1650. If you're prepping for a shorter distance, just adapt my routine to suit.

Several days before, I begin to think about what it will feel like if I'm willing to take it to the limit and not back off in the race when the body starts imploring me to. Will this be a redline effort or something less? Redline, of course.

Come competition day I get in the mood with a long, easy, preevent warmup—typically at least 40 to 45 minutes for a race that takes less than half as long. This does several things. First, just swimming smoothly and easily takes the nervous edge off. Second, you can use the warmup to groove your stroke into what coaches call easy speed, a relaxed, familiar rhythm, a feeling of being controlled and effortless at your projected race pace. It takes at least several minutes to get that, but I don't want to spend the first 500 of my 1650 groping around for it, so I rehearse the feeling now.

And I rehearse until it's right, maybe six or eight 100-yard repeats —nearly half the distance of the race itself—trying to hit target pace precisely on each with that buoyant feeling of easy speed. To race 16 identically paced 100s, you have to go a little harder on each as a new layer of fatigue settles into your muscles. The first few will feel nearly effortless, the last ones will feel like you're lifting a piano. If I can hit six or eight of these with 15 to 20 seconds of rest between, I'm more confident that once the gun goes off, I'll be able to reel off 16 in a row, with no rest, at the same pace.

You'll probably feel better in the early stages of a distance race if you finish your warmup/rehearsal just before your heat starts. There's something to be said for going right from the warmup pool to the starting blocks, with your muscles prepared and your race rhythms all set. Done correctly, a long warmup like this right before the race gives you a net gain in the gas tank, since what you've been practicing is energy conservation.

You've also been setting that confidence-building "clock in the head," the coach's term for an unerring sense of pace. Pool racing is done one to a lane, so there's no such thing as drafting behind anyone. And you might not want to try even if you could. The 1650 is too long to try to swim someone else's race. You perform far better when you do it the way *you've* trained for it. That means having a goal time in mind, and a pace plan for reaching it.

Finally it's time to race. When the gun goes off and you dive in after this kind of prepwork, you'll become quite calm. From the first, your stroke feels just the way you want it to. Now's the time to be patient. For the first 400 to 500 yards (16 to 20 lengths), avoid racing. You're stalking. Keep your stroke as long as possible and your stroke rate as low as possible, and stay within striking distance of your rivals. Everything goes into efficiency, so it's indelibly imprinted onto your nervous system and the coming fatigue and racing pressures can't break it down.

Whatever you do, stay out of oxygen debt. You're excited. You may be trying to keep up. It's too easy to overswim the first part of any race and slip across the anaerobic threshold. Once you do, the only way to recover will be to slow down, and once you've slackened the pace, it's nearly impossible to push it all the way up again. Oh, eventually you'll have to go anaerobic just to hold onto your pace, but you want that to come as near the end of the race as possible. Stay aerobic for three-quarters of the race, and you'll have what it takes in the tanks for the last few 100s.

Eventually, you'll be playing a cat-and-mouse game with fatigue. In a sheer act of will, you try to keep your stroke long, but as you get a little more tired your only recourse is to increase stroke rate—carefully. Do this with hip rolling, not muscle power. (Your muscles don't have that much to spare by now anyhow.) Try to dial it up just a little on each 100 to exactly offset fatigue. It's a delicate game, but if you've practiced enough, you can play it successfully.

You're up to about 1,200 yards now, but who's counting? The answer is, friends are. At the end of the pool opposite the starting blocks, a card showing the lap number is shoved in front of your face just before every turn. This race takes so much concentration that it's impossible to keep track of your lap count, so a friend kneels at the end of your lane and obligingly shoves those numbered cards into the water, shouting encouragement as you turn.

You're closing in now. The last 16 to 20 lengths, and it's time to really bear down. Begin to count. The card reads 51, you're headed into lap 52, and you're thinking, "Only fourteen to go—I can bring this home."

Time to find out what you're made of. No matter how easily you swam the beginning, no matter how intelligent your pace in the middle, your whole body will start to ache for oxygen over the last few hundred yards. Every flip turn seems like an aerobic slap in the face, since the flip turn cuts off your oxygen for a few seconds at each wall. Great. Just what you need. An open turn with your face above water would be so nice, but it costs precious fractions at each wall and you didn't come this far to throw time away now. Too bad it seems like you need the whole length to get your breath back from every turn and just when you have, you get slapped down again.

"Eight lengths to go. Now six. Now just four." Each 50 gets harder but each brings you closer to relief. Finally, you pour everything you have left into the last two lengths, thrust your hand to the touch pad, and it's over!

For a couple of minutes even hanging exhausted on the gutter will hurt, as lactic acid pools in the muscles that generated it. So push off and swim a few massaging laps of easy backstroke to wash some of it out. You're finished. You've taken your Total Immersion training into the contest and proven that even when the rest of the body falters, your muscles can go on autopilot if you've trained them well.

And for me at least, racing like this is an exercise in self-discovery. My final time interests me less than the broader revelation of how well my training has prepared me to race on this particular day. I'm more curious about testing my abilities to execute a good race plan than in what color medal I may have won. And every race I swim presents its own set of lessons which I am always eager to apply when I return to the pool for my next practice.

Chapter 13

Training Aids: The Good, the Not-Bad,
and the Useless

Make no mistake about it. You can become an excellent swimmer with nothing more than your own body, a swimsuit, and some smart coaching. No accessories necessary.

But there are plenty available. Some of them are actually helpful. Kickboards may be the most familiar to newer swimmers, followed closely by fins. But hand paddles, pull buoys, ankle straps, elastic tethers—all beckon with the promise of greater strength or more impressive speed. They supposedly work like Nautilus machines of the water, letting you isolate a movement or muscle you need to work on, then bear down on it with concentrated training.

Some do. Others at least won't do you any harm. And still others sound good but are a waste of time at best and an actual detriment to your swimming at worst.

By the time we're done with this chapter, you'll know which ones fit into your Total Immersion program as genuine improvement aids and which ones are best left on the pool deck.

Take kickboards, those light foam slabs everyone loves to hate. We go right on using them because we think that they're probably good for us, like a powerful cough medicine with a nasty taste. I don't necessarily agree. And one of the surefire applause winners in every one of my weekend workshops is the session on training aids, when I announce to campers that they'll be better off if they never pick up a kickboard again. Next thing I know, I'm looking into the kind of happy faces that must have greeted the Allies on D-Day. These people have been chugging up and down the pool for what seems like their whole lives, working on a weak kick but getting nowhere, figuring the stalemate had to be their fault for not doing something right.

"Now," some of them happily figure, "I can spend more time with fun things like buoys, paddles, and fins." Almost everyone swims faster with those right away—and you don't even have to work any harder! Put any of them on and suddenly, it seems, this improvement stuff's a breeze.

But that's not necessarily true either. With many, the magic lasts only while you're wearing the gear. The moment you take it off, you're right back where you started.

Why are their effects so temporary? Simple. Because many pool tools simply mask your worst stroke errors, doing nothing to correct them. Total Immersion is all about improving your stroke, not improving how you swim with a bad one, so let's state Laughlin's Rule on Pool Tools right now: "Spend lots of time kicking with a kickboard and you'll become better at . . . kicking with a kickboard. And pulling with buoys and paddles mainly makes you better at pulling with buoys and paddles." Not quite the kind of improvement you were looking for, is it?

No matter how much time you spend using them, there's little chance training aids will improve your swimming unless you know just how they can help you, limit your time with them, and avoid becoming dependent.

So let's find out how to do all that.

Kickboards and Fins

Kickboards, those tombstone-shaped foam slabs, are a common instrument of swimming torture embraced by discouraged athletes who think that a weak kick is holding them back because their hips and legs drag. So, they figure, the solution must be to strengthen the legs. Surely enough mind-numbing laps on the board will do that.

They won't, for two reasons. First, if your hips and legs are dragging it's probably poor balance and not a poor kick that's to blame. We've already shown how easily that's corrected, and kicking has next to nothing to do with it. When you press your buoy or swim downhill, your rear end will ride up where it belongs. Even a weak kick can't hold back a balanced body. In fact, once you get balanced, you probably won't even *need* to kick.

Where a stronger kick does come in handy is in gaining speed after you've improved your balance. But kickboard work can't even promise you this, because if your legs are to move you faster they must be not only strong but flexible. Elite swimmers kick so powerfully because their ankles are so supple. Most of them can sit on the deck, legs out in front and knees straight, and touch their toes to the floor in front of them. The rest of us are lucky if we can go half that far, though it's by no means certain, by the way, that we should all set out to achieve it. Hypermobility (unusual ranges of flexibility) in any joint comes at the cost of diminished joint stability. A highly flexible ankle on someone who runs, for example, is an ankle sprain waiting to happen. So even though step one to kicking better is ankle stretching, don't overdo it if you run or play squash, tennis, basketball, or any other sport with a lot of cutting from side to side.

Stronger legs are step two. But kickboard sets still aren't the answer. It's true that they will make your legs stronger, but not the way you're hoping. The movements at which you'll be stronger are not the ones you swim with. Think about it. Remember, hip roll is your power source—for swimming *and* kicking. But on a kickboard, your hips are locked into place. The interaction of hip and leg muscles is changed so that whatever leg strength you might be building is kickboard-kicking strength, not swim-kicking strength.

The best way to put flexibility *and* muscle into a weak kick? Fins, for two reasons. First, the extra pressure created by the blade on each downbeat stretches the foot more than a "naked" kick does. Second, the increased surface area of the blade puts a greater load on your leg muscles. It's like a wet weight workout.

Doing your Total Immersion swim drills with fins can help you achieve even more. Drills force you to use your legs more than you do when swimming, so they'll get stronger with the fins, and it will be strength you can *use* because the drills so closely approximate the real swim stroke. Plus, you'll be improving your stroke efficiency.

The two best ways to do this are side-lying kick and slide & glide drills. On both of these you're kicking on your side so the fin blade stays completely underwater, where increased pressure gives your legs a better workout.

You can wear fins on some of your swimming sets, but not more than about 10 percent of them, please. You'll be tempted to do more. The plain truth is, most of us don't kick very much when we swim because it really doesn't help all that much. And the farther we swim, the less we kick. But with fins, the speed payback is obvious. Every kick is like a little supercharged burst. So kicking is now clearly worth the effort, and you build strength you can use in swimming because that's exactly how you got it.

Know, however, that all fins are not created equal. There are different designs, good for different types of swimmers. The so-called "speed" fins or Zoomers have a small blade and work best for skilled swimmers who already have good ankle flexibility and a strong kick and are interested mainly in short sprints with a high stroke rate. If you're more interested in developing skill and stamina, you'll do better with the extra area of a bladed fin. I happen to think the best designed among those is the Slim Fin.

So if all you want for your time today is a good leg workout of no specific value, grab your tombstone . . . er, kickboard, and be my guest. But if you're looking for strength that can help move you down the lane smoothly, leave the kickboard on the pool deck. More fin-driven drilling is your answer.

Buoys and Paddles

Unlike kickboards, people love to use these. Some won't even take them off. After all, you're so much faster with buoys and paddles than you are in just plain old swimming that it's hard to go back. And that may not be all bad. If you're interested simply in an aerobic workout, you can get a fine one wearing buoys and paddles. But if you're wearing them to learn *swimming,* then put them aside.

That may be especially hard in the case of pull buoys, a pair of foam cylinders connected by nylon rope, which don't work the way most people have been taught to think they work. The common misconception is that buoys make your pull stronger by overloading your arms. Just the opposite is true. The foam makes you float higher, which *under*loads your arms by supporting those mulish hips and legs of yours that are still fighting your buoy-pressing to the end. So the buoy just masks your problem. Until the day when race officials let you swim with your buoy, you'll be better off learning to fix that imbalance by swimming downhill instead.

However, there is a way to strengthen your arms using a buoy: Add paddles to your hands and a tube around your ankles to the buoy between your legs. That will both increase the resistance and add some muscle to your pull.

But paddles are not perfect either. If you're going to use them for strength training, you'd better be sure you have a model stroke. If not, you're asking for a shoulder strain as the added work the muscles must do to pull that paddle blade through the water gets taken up by the wrong muscles and joints. If your stroke is still less than picture-perfect, use paddles not for strength but for 1. developing a *longer* stroke, and 2. becoming better at front-quadrant swimming by learning to reach farther forward after your entry before pulling back, both of which they encourage. The extra surface area of the paddle makes you more aware of what your hand is doing, including whether or not you're sliding it forward to full extension.

Use them too as tutors for a more efficient pull. Remember, you're not supposed to be pushing water past your body to move yourself, you're to hold onto the water and *pull yourself past your hand.* So you want to feel like you're holding on as your body slides by, and the best way to tell if you're doing it right is to make sure your hand never moves back faster than your body is moving forward. Swimming with paddles is probably the best way to understand how this should feel.

That's why I recommend "Swiss cheese" paddles, the ones with holes that let the water through to your hand, rather than the solid plastic ones. After all, if the paddle's most important function is to improve your feel for the water, you might as well feel it. Those holes also reduce the load the paddles put on your shoulder joint, which in turn reduces your risk of injury. And if your paddles come with a wrist strap, take it off. Use only the strap that holds the paddle at your fingers and you'll automatically keep the proper water pressure. If you don't, the paddle falls off. A wrist strap lets you get away with too much.

Between improving your front-quadrant swimming and holding water better, you should take at least one or two fewer strokes per length with paddles. Just remember that the real point is to eventually do the same thing without them. Don't confuse the process with the end result, and limit your use of paddles to not more than 10 percent of your total swimming yardage. Most of your time should still be devoted to swimming with the equipment nature gave you.

Webbed Swim Gloves

Leave these to the aqua-aerobicizers. Anything they could do for your stroke, paddles will do much better.

Swim Benches

Swim benches like the Vasa Swim Trainer and the Simuswim, devices you lie on face down while moving your arms in a swimminglike motion against a resistance, have become much more technologically advanced than when they first came out. Their manufacturers are making claims for them that are pretty advanced too: Perfect your stroke, get total-body conditioning, get as much from your "swim" at home as you could going to the pool, etc. They have to make such claims because the benches will set you back from 600 to 2,000 dollars. My advice is, save your money.

I don't say that because of the price; I say it from personal experience. I began using a swim bench 30 years ago to strengthen my arms for swimming. It was a simple affair with a handle, rope, and pulley system for lifting weights with a swimming motion. I was sure it made my arms stronger. And I was equally sure that would improve my swimming.

Today, I'm still convinced that exercising on a swim bench can make your arms stronger. But now that I understand the dynamics of the stroke better, I'm no longer convinced it will improve your swimming.

A body moving through water and a body lying on a bench simply do not behave the same way. The biomechanical action (the way different muscle groups interact) and the kinesthetics (your muscle sense) are entirely different. So swim bench workouts train you to do swim bench workouts. If you're planning to enter swim bench competition, then by all means get yourself one of these. If you'd like to swim better, save your money for real training in a real pool—swim instruction, swim videos or books, fins, paddles, Masters Swimming membership, almost anything will give you a bigger bang for your buck. If you must have something at home to supplement your swimming, you can get a device that sells for about 5 percent of what the least expensive swim bench costs, yet will provide 90 percent of its benefit. It's called a stretchcord. Please read on.

Stretchcords

Stretchcords are lengths of latex tubing with handles at each end and a nylon loop in the middle which can anchor the cord to a wide variety of fixed objects—table legs, doorknobs, radiators, anything strong and stable. They come in various thicknesses allowing you to match your individual strength level.

Cords have been one of my favorite training aids for over 20 years because they're the most affordable and versatile of any strength-building tool that can legitimately be recommended for swimmers. In fact, a 1989 study at the University of New Brunswick in Canada found that a daily stretchcord workout of 20 minutes (12 to 14 minutes of exercise, six to eight minutes of rest) helped swimmers hang on to virtually all of their conditioning during a three-week layoff.

Like swim benches, the stretchcord movement is different from swimming—but not that much different, and this time your investment is only 30 to 35 dollars. Besides, stretchcord exercises are easily modified for a great variety of benefits and sports. Swim coaches like cords because they give you the same steady, fluid resistance that water does. Cords also let you work through a virtually endless range of motion, limited only by your joints and your workout space.

If you work out in the weight room to build swimming strength, you should also be working out with stretchcords. They act as an effective and necessary bridge between nonspecific strength work in the weight room and swim-specific movement in the pool. Weight training builds muscles, of course, but it builds them just the way you work while doing a bench press, a lat pulldown, a bent-over row, etc. Swimming uses those muscles differently and always in a low-load situation. Stretchcord training helps translate your weight room strength to pool strength by working your muscles in swimming-specific motions, but under much higher loads than water could provide.

Finally, cords can be easily used for "prehab" exercise to correct muscle imbalances caused by swimming, and to strengthen the shoulder joint to protect against tendinitis and other injuries. In fact, physical therapists prescribe stretchcord exercises to rehab many shoulder injuries.

Swim Flumes and Tethers

If you just can't stand having that extra $14,000 burning a hole in your pocket for another minute, install a swim flume (Endless Pool is one brand name) in your house and save yourself the time and trouble of going to the Y.

Or you could save your money for some better use, which is what I would suggest. A swim flume, basically a 15-foot-long, three-foot-deep bathtub with a water current circulating in the front end and out the back, is a way to swim upstream and go nowhere. As with most everything else we've discussed in this chapter, you can indeed use it to get a workout (though an extraordinarily monotonous one). But it will do nothing to make you a better swimmer. Your stroke moving forward through still water is dramatically different from your stroke when you're trying to hold yourself in place in a stream of water that's moving by you. And none of the difference is helpful.

Worst of all, no matter how hard you swim you'll go backward—in the skills sense, that is. You'll forget about gliding your body and about sliding your hand forward. You'll also lose any semblance of a front-quadrant stroke since in a moving current your hand will have to enter, grab water, and pull it back in a hurry to keep you from being pushed to the back of the flume. Not good. Not only are you teaching your muscles lessons in *inefficient* swimming, you can easily develop shoulder problems after awhile. So stay out of flumes.

Swim tethers are just about as bad, at least if they hold you in place. A swim tether is a longer stretchcord that you attach between you and a fixed object at the end of your lane. Some are only long enough to allow you to move perhaps 10 yards down the pool before halting your progress. Then you stroke in place at the end of your gigantic rubber band for however long you want—perfect, some people feel, for training in a short backyard or hotel pool.

The idea sounds reasonable enough, letting you do your workout in a fraction of the space. But unfortunately you're not doing yourself much more good than if you'd spent that $14,000 on the swim flume, because you're just holding your body in place against the constant backward pull of your tether.

On the other hand, a swim tether that's long enough to let you swim all the way to the end of the pool (for a 25-yard pool this would be about 30 feet of relatively light tubing) can help you accomplish some useful things. Called a Longbelt, it lets you swim against gradually increasing resistance—the last five yards can be very tough—and you're moving forward the whole time.

The best thing you can do while wearing a swim tether is count your strokes, work on reducing your strokes per length (the total will obviously be different with something pulling your legs backward), and play swimming golf. Use a sports watch to time yourself, add your stroke count to your time, and you have a score. On subsequent Longbelt lengths, work on reducing it.

You can even practice sprinting. After you get all the way to the far end, rest at the wall (hang on tight!) for a moment, then turn around and swim back as fast as you can, the belt pulling you along faster than you could ever swim all by yourself. This is called sprint-assisted training, and it teaches your muscles to move faster than your best race pace.

But if you're working on your stroke count or your golf score, just float lazily back to the starting end, letting the cord do all the work. In just a minute, you'll need the energy you're saving to fight your way back down the pool again.

Two things you can say about swim training aids: You don't necessarily get what you pay for, and an idea that sounds good on paper or in ad copy doesn't necessarily make sense to your body. The simplest pool tools seem to work the best. And never forget that the simplest one of all remains your own body.

PART THREE

Swimming for Life:
Be Healthy, Be Strong,
Be Happy—Here's How

Chapter 14

Swimming the Pounds Away

"Swimming? Absolutely the best all-around exercise. But if you want to lose weight, you need to run."

A lot of people still believe this, and a lot of people are wrong. It's an issue of more than passing interest to anyone who wants to shed a few pounds and prefers to spend most of his or her available exercise time in the pool. Actually, there's no scientific reason to be discouraged, and there's every reason to take heart.

Swimming has long suffered from a bad rep—especially compared to running and cycling—when it comes to weight control. "Great exercise but no fat-burner," repeat the skeptics, driving people unnecessarily onto the pavement in search of trimmer bodies. And you can understand how an unscientific sampling could seem to prove this. Just look at the number of gaunt runners slipping through the streets

on a Saturday morning. Everyday athletes, not even elite champions.

But let's get scientific for a minute. The real question is, do swimming workouts burn as many calories—and as much fat—as running or biking? Several studies over the past few years have suggested that they do not. But in each case the deck was stacked experimentally. The flaw common to all the studies was that the swimming, and the running to which it was compared, were not done at the same intensities. The swimming paces were far too slow to provide a reliable comparison.

Then, a 1989 study at the University of California at Davis finally compared the weight loss effects of running and swimming on two groups, both of whom exercised at identical intensities: 75 percent of maximum capacity for every subject in both sports. And what do you suppose happened? The swimmers not only lost as much weight as the runners, they actually lost slightly more.

And four years later, Howard Wainer, a Princeton, New Jersey, swimmer who also happens to be a statistician calculated that champion swimmers burn about 25 percent *more* calories per hour than champion runners. Wainer's study, published in *Chance,* the journal of the American Statistical Association, suggested that swimming takes more energy because the drag forces of water are so much greater than air resistance on land, and also because swimmers work so many more muscles than runners.

Swimmers, of course, found none of this surprising. People who know the sport realize that elite swimmers are just as lean as elite athletes in any other sport. They simply look bigger than top runners, for example, because they *are* bigger. Fast swimming requires a powerful upper body, so swimmers' arm, chest, and back muscles are typically far more developed than those of runners or even cyclists.

So equal work produces equally lean bodies among serious athletes in swimming and other sports. But what about the obvious weight differences between casual swimmers and casual runners? In part, I'm convinced, it's a matter of simple psychology. Since your body weight in water is only 10 percent of what it is on land, an overweight runner feels every extra pound with every single step, while a chunky swimmer can be supremely comfortable. So, who has more motivation to watch what goes onto the plate?

Researchers have a more scientific explanation for the same eating behavior. Swimmers usually weigh more not because they burn fewer calories than other athletes, but because they *consume* more, says a study done by Dr. Grant Gwinup at the University of California at Irvine Medical Center. Gwinup's reasoning: Water at, say, 78 degrees

Fahrenheit draws much more heat from the body than air at the same temperature. And swimmers' bodies react to that by adding protective insulation, which of course requires food to build up. My personal experience convinces me Dr. Gwinup is right. I never feel like eating after a run, while after swimming, I'm always primed to strap on the feedbag.

However, elite athlete or no, several strategies can help you both burn more fat while swimming *and* depress your post-swim-workout appetite when you're done. First, stay full-feeling simply by staying well hydrated (see "Hydration: When Swimmers Run Out of Water" on page 212). Drink ample fluids during the workout, which you should be doing anyway. Second, allow yourself some judicious snacking on filling but low-fat foods (such as fruit, or fig bars) immediately after your swimming workout. That will tame your stoked-up appetite without piling on pounds.

How—and even when—you swim can affect the amount of fat you end up burning. During intense exercise, your muscles must rely on a very limited supply of stored energy. But swim at a moderate effort and that all changes. Though it takes longer to burn the same number of calories at a slower pace, a greater percentage of the fuel being used is fat.

And physiologists now believe we can actually train our bodies to burn more fat even at higher intensities. The crossover point is usually somewhere around 60 percent of an all-out effort—fairly low, actually—after which our burners switch over to carbohydrates as we work harder. But with the right training we can keep fat going into the furnace at efforts as high as 70 or even 80 percent of maximum.

Do this: Schedule a long swim practice (60 to 90 minutes or even more) after eight to twelve hours of carbohydrate deprivation. The easiest way is to plan your workouts for the morning, before breakfast.

By swimming easily for 60 to 90 minutes you'll burn more stored fat (Total Immersion intervals can do this as well as nonstop swimming can—they just have to be *easy* intervals), and the more you repeat this routine, the more you'll condition your body to use fat rather than stored muscle energy (called glycogen) as fuel.

Need more of a carrot to do that much work on an empty stomach? Here it is: That University of California at Davis study also showed that prolonged, easy aerobic training sessions give you an impressive afterburn, boosting your metabolism so you continue burning extra calories for up to 12 hours after you finish your workout.

Bottom line: you *can* lose weight in the pool. Any swimmer having trouble with the pounds ought to blame his fork, not his sport.

Hydration: When Swimmers Run Out of Water

Earlier in this book, I promised you could become a very good swimmer with nothing more than your suit, cap, and goggles. No added equipment necessary.

Not quite. One piece of equipment should always be sitting on the deck at the end of your lane: your water bottle. It's easy, and common, to mistakenly figure that because your sweat isn't obvious, it's not happening. But you not only sweat during a swim workout, you sweat copiously.

Prove it by weighing yourself before and after a workout. You've lost weight, of course, and it's all water. Sweat losses of as little as two percent of your body weight (just 3 lbs. for a 150-lb. swimmer) can cut dramatically into your performance. In fact, dehydration is far more likely to slow you down than running out of muscle energy, making "water loading" even more important than carbo loading.

But plain water is not always the liquid of choice. A study by Dr.

Jack Wilmore, an exercise physiologist at the University of Texas, found that for workouts of less than an hour, nothing beats water. If you're going longer, fluid replacement sports drinks that contain electrolytes (salts) are absorbed into your bloodstream faster than water, which means better performance and a faster recovery when you're done.

Their formulas are all slightly different, so I can only repeat the standard coach's advice: experiment. Some may agree with you and others may not. I found one that tastes good to me and sits well in my stomach, and I've noticed a marked boost during the second half of any 75-minute workout since I've started using it.

The Smart Swimmer's Drinking Rules

1. You can sweat off six to eight ounces of fluid every 15 minutes—yes, even in the pool. That's a healthy swig from your water bottle every quarter-hour.
2. Want to be more precise? Weigh yourself before and after a workout. Each pound lost is a pint (16 ounces) of water gone out of you. Next time, bring that much in your water bottle(s).
3. Prehydrate. Drink two to three cups of water about two hours before swimming and another two cups 15 minutes before your workout.
4. Drink *before* you're thirsty. Thirst means your body already needs water, so it's too late to prevent dehydration. This is especially true for older swimmers, since after middle age we feel less thirsty as we dry out and the body's warning signals can be overlooked.

Shedding Pounds in the Pool:
How to Swim to Burn the Most Fat

Is swimming an effective exercise for losing weight? It certainly is, despite all the theories to the contrary that have come and gone. We now know this: If you burn more calories than you eat, you will drop pounds—on an exercise bike, at the track, or in the pool. And swimming is one of the most comfortable ways to burn calories you'll ever find.

So if slimming down by reducing body fat, improving your cholesterol count, and helping lower blood pressure are important goals for your exercise program, you've come to the right sport. And believe it or not the best way to do all of that, plus improve your stroke technique, is with easy swimming, the keystone of Total Immersion swimming.

Recent research has proven that exercising moderately (at just 60 percent of your maximum heart rate) provides the same health benefits as hard workouts as long as you cover the same distance. That's health, mind you, in contrast to performance. Obviously if you want to win a championship by swimming faster than everyone else, you'll still have to do intense work. But it's not an essential ingredient to keeping your cardiovascular system tuned up.

In a six-month study at the Cooper Institute for Aerobics Research in Dallas, a group of women who walked three miles daily at a slow pace gained the same health benefits as a group that walked the same distance much faster. In fact, walking burns just as many calories per mile as running. It just takes longer to cover the same distance.

Michael Pollock, Ph.D., Director of the Human Performance Laboratory at the University of Florida, found that slow walking was also just as effective as fast walking at reducing body fat, high blood pressure, and cholesterol. And at the Cooper Institute, the strollers actually lost more body fat than the power walkers.

None of this is surprising, since researchers have long known the best way to burn fat is to exercise at lower intensities for longer periods of time. Our bodies use two main fuels to supply energy: fats (which we'd like to burn more of), and carbohydrates (which our bodies, left to their own devices, would like to burn more of; carbohydrates are more efficient, after all). Long, easy workouts are one way to get the body to draw a greater percentage of the energy it needs from fats than it would if you sped things up.

''The total amount of work you do ends up being the important factor,'' says Pollock. ''People can go slower. They just need to go longer to get the same results.''

Well, that's certainly easy enough. If you swim a mile at an average pace of 1:30 per 100 yards, you'll finish the workout in only 27 minutes. At 2:00 per 100 yards, you'll be done in 36 minutes. But you obviously can't cut back both pace *and* distance. Less is less. Even the American College of Sports

continued

Swimming the Pounds Away — — — — — — — — — —

Medicine, which now advises that it's OK to work at less than 60 percent of maximal capacity, stipulates that you must still do it long enough and frequently enough to get the benefit. For adult swimmers, this would mean about 6,000 to 8,000 yards of swimming a week, in 3 to 4 pool sessions.

So there's nothing wrong with discovering that easing your pace a little makes it easier to get to the pool in the first place. Higher-intensity exercise programs inevitably suffer from higher dropout rates because people just don't enjoy them and get frustrated when they can't "measure up." "By encouraging slower, more comfortable exercise," says Dr. Pollock, "we're giving people a reason *to* exercise rather than an excuse not to."

No argument from me. After all, easy swimming is also the perfect pace for Total Immersion swimming. You can do your drills and technique work and count your strokes per length much more effectively at low intensity than when you're trying to burn up the pool.

Even interval training, normally done with a little more gusto, can become a "fat-burner." Just use a more relaxed pace. You won't need much rest between repeats because your heart rate will stay fairly even at moderate paces, but even brief rests are beneficial—especially for adult swimmers—since they control the levels of fatigue-producing lactic acid that accumulates in muscles and the bloodstream. That in turn means less stiffness and soreness after your workout. And interval repeats with their built-in rest periods help the heart supply more blood, oxygen, and nutrients to joints and muscles, reducing your chance of hurting something.

But how fast is "slow enough"? To calculate your easygoing, pound-dropping, health-building clip for intervals, multiply your best 100-yard time by anywhere from 1.25 to 1.5. So if your best time is 1:20, you'll be right on target at a pace between 1:40 and 2:00 per 100. Plan on 10 to 20 seconds of rest between swims. And if you're doing stroke drills rather than straight swimming, your times will naturally fall in the upper part of the range. Use the same formula to figure your pace for repeats of other distances. Or just follow the Total Immersion practices in the appendix. Done as suggested, they work well as both stroke-builders and fat-burners.

To enjoy the optimum fat-burning benefit, just add enough repeats or sets to allow for at least an hour in the pool. But as you do so, keep in mind the potential conflict between longer sessions (to burn more fat) and quality skill work (to become a better swimmer). If you can't maintain good form for an hour or more, you may have to choose one priority over another. If it's becoming a better swimmer, don't stretch the practice to the point where fatigue hurts your form, just so you can burn a few more calories. Instead add 30 minutes of walking or biking or treadmill or exercise bike or anything which simply burns calories and fat, yet isn't dependent on maintaining good form.

Chapter 15

What to Do in the Weight Room:
Strength Training the Total Immersion Way

In Total Immersion swimming, there's no such thing as "pumping up." That's partly because—as I've said over and over—skill will always outdistance strength in the water. But it's also partly because the strength training that swimmers should do is different from the ordinary circuit of machines or free weights, at least initially. That kind of resistance training works by building bulk, and bulk is something swimmers don't need. Beautiful muscles by themselves may get dates and make mirrors happy, but they have little to do with moving you down the pool.

The strength you build with, say, some mighty bench presses is mostly strength that lets you do more mighty bench presses. What you need, instead, is sport-specific muscle power, in this case power to swim with. It's commonly called functional strength, and it becomes more and more important to develop as the years go by.

This is true no matter how much you work out in the pool. Swimming may be a more complete exercise than either running or cycling, but it doesn't build serious muscle because buoyancy decreases the work our bodies have to do in the water. And muscle tissue is important not just because it's what moves you but because it's also your body's calorie-burning engine, consuming more than any other type of tissue. So the more muscle you build, the more calories you burn—even when you're not working out.

But neglected muscle tissue is not inclined to stick around, which is one reason people tend to gain weight—and fat—as they get older. We lose about half a pound of calorie-burning muscle each year after age 30, partly because of biological factors we can't reverse but largely because of lack of activity which we *can* reverse. In fact there's now an official prescription for adults approaching or already in middle age, from no less a fitness think tank than the American College of Sports Medicine. They say all adults need two weekly sessions of high-repetition, moderate-resistance strength training, no matter how much aerobic work they're doing.

Weight training can not only help us become stronger swimmers and keep the pounds off, it can also reduce the risk of injury. Swimmers' "prime mover" muscles (the ones that pull the arm down) tend to become overdeveloped, while the "antagonist" muscles (the ones that lift the arm) remain weak. Likewise, the "internal rotator" muscles that pull the arms together develop more than the "external rotators" that pull them apart. These muscle imbalances increase the chance of shoulder strains. And many so-called swimming-specific weight training programs make matters even worse because they tend to focus on the already overdeveloped muscle groups, increasing the imbalance and the chance of injury.

There is a better way, certainly in the early stages of any swimming-strength-training program you may be starting. It's a way that's more convenient, more economical, and safer than weight training with equipment. It's training that simply uses your own body for resistance —bodyweight exercises, they're usually called. Vern Gambetta, Director of Conditioning for the Chicago White Sox, is a big advocate of both functional-strength and bodyweight exercises to achieve it. He believes, and I agree with him, that athletes rush too quickly to machines when they decide their muscles need work. "The mistake people make, especially older adult athletes, is to work with machines first," Gambetta declares. "That takes away balance, joint stability, and muscle sense. Most machines work our bodies in two planes, like a hinge. But that's not how we move in sports."

Anxious to build big muscles, we don't ask first what good the conditioning is supposed to do us. Do we want to look great in photos or out on the field? The answer should be the latter, because it's functional strength, not cosmetics, that will make us better athletes, more robust in everything we do from spading the garden to swimming a 1500. And *that* means training muscles and joints to work in all the planes in which they move, not isolating them into one plane as happens with most weight machines. It also means building joint stability before muscle strength.

We usually do just the opposite, according to Gambetta. "Say I'm a serious forty-year-old swimmer, or maybe a triathlete, who does 1,500 to 2,000 yards a day and supplements that with bench presses to strengthen my pectoral muscles," he says, giving a typical example. "What I'm doing is developing my prime-mover muscles without first conditioning the ones that stabilize the joint they attach to. Pretty soon I'll have tendinitis in my shoulder because it's just not balanced." Stability before strength, always.

Pinpointing and building up specific muscles, which is what machines do so well, is the last thing you want when you're building a strength base, according to Gambetta. "When you use an arm-curl machine, you're training your biceps muscle. But you should really be training elbow flexion. The muscles all work together synergistically." And the more you replicate the way the body moves, the more you'll build strength in the way you'll use it.

So exercise it that way, Gambetta declares. No machines or free weights in the beginning, just working the old-fashioned way. "You've got to be able to handle your own bodyweight before you work with external resistance. Exercises like push-ups, pull-ups, dips, step-ups, done with just the weight of your own body, give you the muscle sense and joint stability you need at the start. They also let your tendons and ligaments adapt in ways machines can't." And the greater the exercise variety, the more you're working the joints in just the ways you'll actually use them later.

One more thing if you're looking for functional strength. A body that can *use* its power—rather than a body with powerful but not especially useful arms and legs—is a body that also has *core* strength. The core is the torso, in Gambetta's definition, "the center of the body. But it's more than the abdominal muscles. It's also the spinal rotators and erectors, hip flexors, the glutes, and more. If the core isn't strong then neither are you, because that's the force couple, the transmission that transfers power to the limbs." Swimmers might even try core exercises as part of their warmups before jumping into the pool, because it's the core that transfers to the upper body the power generated by hip roll.

Since you should work on core strength before limb strength, it's fortunate the body is a willing partner in building it. "Most of the core-strength muscles are antigravity muscles. That means you're using them all the time, since gravity never takes a day off, so they're relatively well conditioned. That means they recover rapidly after a workout, and you can work them more often, more than the legs or upper body," says Gambetta.

Eventually, of course, your muscles will need more than body-weight to continue growing stronger. So after about two months of the exercise plan on the next page, begin mixing in resistance training (free weights or machines) in equal amounts.

Prepped this way, using the exercise plan, you'll be ready at last to venture to the weight room. With well-prepared, stable, and strong joints, increasing the power that pulls on them will no longer be so risky. And once you're there, I can tell you that there's no secret

Throwing Your Weight Around
A Basic Bodyweight Exercise Program

Begin with one set and go to five by adding one set each week. Do at least two exercises from each scheduled category.

I. Upper Body

▶ Push-ups: 20 reps (Can be modified; if you can't do 20 in the strict military position, do them from your knees or with hands on a bench to lessen the load.)

▶ Pull-ups: Test for maximum, then train at 50 percent of maximum reps.

▶ Bench or Bar Dips: 20 reps.

II. Core

▶ Three-position sit-ups: 5 reps (With knees bent, feet flat on floor, hands behind head, sit up and twist right, back down, sit up and twist left, back down, sit up to center, back down; that's one rep.)

▶ Curl-ups: 10 reps (Lie on small of back, knees bent, feet flat on floor, fingertips lightly touching ears. Curl just your shoulder blades off the ground, then back down.)

▶ Russian twists: 20 reps (Bent-leg sit-up position with feet flat on floor, torso half-raised, arms straight forward, palms together; twist side to side.)

III. Legs

▶ Single-leg squat: 5 reps each leg (Hand on a chair for balance, bend "resting" leg up behind you, lower down to a comfortable position, then back up.)

continued

What to Do in the Weight Room: Total Immersion Strength Training

- Bodyweight squat: 20 reps (Touch fingertips to ears, keep back straight, [raise chin slightly to help posture]; lower slowly to full squat, then return.)

- Lunges: 20 reps (10 each leg) (Hands on hips, step forward with one leg until the knee of the back leg nearly touches the floor, then back up.)

- Step-ups: 20 reps (10 each leg) (Use a bench about knee high or lower; leave one foot on bench, step up until other foot is at bench height, then lower to touch floor. Complete 10 with one leg, then switch.)

- Jump squats: 15 reps (Jump up as high as possible from a squatting position.)

IV. Total Body

- Treadmill: 20 reps (Like running in the push-up position. Leg forward/leg back equals one rep.)

- Burpee: 10 reps (Squat with hands flat on floor, thrust legs straight out, pull legs back in, stand up, repeat.)

Weekly Distribution (two week cycles)

	Monday	Tuesday	Wednesday	Thursday	Friday	Saturday	Sunday
Week 1, 3, 5, etc.	Category I & II	III	I & II	II	I & II	IV	off
Week 2, 4, 6, etc.	Category I & II	III	IV	II	I & II	off	off

swimming-strength formula I know of. Just find a certified strength-and-conditioning trainer, and ask for a general body-strengthening program that focuses on compound or complex (using more than one joint at a time) rather than single-joint exercises. Then spend enough time under professional supervision to learn proper form and progression before training on your own.

Some people are happy to stay in phase one of "Throwing Your Weight Around" on page 223, and that's fine too. It will certainly build all the strength you need to become an accomplished Total Immersion swimmer.

And you'll be able to do all your workouts anywhere, any time you want. "There's something to be said for needing no equipment," Gambetta says. "The body, after all, is the ultimate free weight."

Chapter 16

Keeping Your Workouts Injury Free

Injury-free swimming? Isn't that redundant, like "fast skydiving" or "tough rugby"? After all, swimming is *supposed* to be injury free, without any extra help from anybody. Just ask all those ex-runners and cyclists who got fed up tearing this tendon and pulling that muscle. They finally settled into the pool, confident that whether or not this sport was their bodies' first love, at least it was a sport that loved their bodies.

I'd be the last to say that swimming doesn't deserve its reputation for being both vigorous and gentle. No pounding, twisting, pressing, snapping, or jerking. Just one weightless, fluid motion after another, like Neil Armstrong on the moon.

But unfortunately, "gentle" cannot promise "injury-free," and though there's no equivalent in the pool to a runner's stress-fractured shin or a skier's torn knee cartilage, there is one joint you have to watch: the shoulder. Caution is necessary for swimmers young and old, because even though adults usually swim far less yardage than youthful competitors, the accumulated strain of years of golf, tennis, softball, or any other overhead sport can still be setting us up for shoulder trouble in the pool.

That's because even with good stroke mechanics, always your first defense against injury, your shoulder joint is all but built to get into trouble. An inherently unstable design, it's like a golf ball (the top of your arm bone) on a tee (the socket the bone fits into), the two pieces held in place by no fewer than 17 different muscles. That fragile engineering does let the arm move in every direction, which is nice, but through continued use the muscles can fatigue and become overstretched. When they do, they allow the humerus (a.k.a. arm bone) to wobble in the joint and possibly pinch the muscles that wrap over the shoulder. How likely is that fatigue? Consider that a swimmer's shoulder rotates 1,200 to 1,500 times every *mile* while a major-league baseball pitcher's may do 1,000 in a *week,* and you can appreciate the need for a little preventive maintenance.

It's worth doing, to avoid that pinching we spoke of. When a fatigued and unstable arm is repeatedly raised or rotated overhead, the tendons can be painfully trapped beneath a tight arch formed by the collarbone and the scapula, or shoulder blade. And a pinched tendon quickly becomes a swollen, inflamed, and painful tendon. Poor stroke mechanics can accelerate the condition, starting a spiral of mounting pain and ebbing strength.

As in so many injuries, the most effective way to deal with swimmer's shoulder is to prevent it. That means a proper warmup before you swim, good stroke mechanics while you are swimming, and a regular maintenance program between swims of stretching and strengthening the connective tissue in the shoulders and rotator cuff. Here's how.

The "Swimmer's Shoulder" Prevention Plan

1. *Get Ready: Warm Up (and Warm Down).* This is one of the simplest preventive measures you can take. Start each workout with five to ten minutes of gentle swimming (or at least 10 percent of your total time or yardage), followed by five minutes or so of on-deck flexibility exercises (see page 229), before beginning your practice with technique work, and your shoulders will be prepared for most any workout. And after a particularly tough practice, the same amount of easy swimming followed by more stretching is like buying extra insurance. It flushes

out accumulated energy waste products from your muscles, eliminates postpractice soreness and tightness, and gets you ready sooner for your next workout. And especially after the all-out stress of racing, a warmdown had better be as much a part of your routine as a hot shower.

2. *Get Smooth: Adjust Your Stroke Mechanics.* Any way you look at it, Total Immersion stroke drills are your first line of defense against shoulder trouble. The drills that get you properly balanced reduce the load on arms that no longer have to drive down urgently into the water to buoy up your torso. When your weight is properly distributed the water does the work, as you'll remember from our discussion of front quadrant swimming and the "weightless arm" (Chapters 3 and 8). That in turn minimizes loading of the joint when it's in its unstable, overhead position. And the drills that emphasize body roll reduce the strain of the recovery action.

Mastering balance and body roll freestyle drills also makes it easier to breathe bilaterally (to both sides), which in turn spreads the work equally between both shoulders. Breathe just to one side all the time, and your opposite shoulder takes more of a beating.

Add a relaxed, high-elbow recovery and a low, sweeping hand movement to your body roll, and you're treating that temperamental "golf ball and tee" joint with the deference it deserves.

3. *Get Supple: Stretch Those Swimming Muscles.* Athletes need to be flexible. So do the rest of us. After all, "flexibility" is just another word for joints that move the way nature intended them to move, instead of growing tighter and stiffer through too much exercise or simple aging, or both. Swimming promotes natural flexibility and fights the stiffness of aging better than any other aerobic activity, but it's not enough all by itself.

Though ever-limber teenagers can just turn the page, the rest of us

Keeping Your Workouts Injury Free — — — — — — — —

probably recognize the signs of swimming too much and stretching too little: a constricting tightness settling into the shoulders, lower back, and legs. I know I can count on it every time I start cheating on my stretching routine.

And having arms and legs of rubber doesn't mean you can skip the flexibility work. Even supple swimmers should stretch. Here's why.

Any exercise shortens and tightens muscles. The more the exercise and the greater its intensity, the stiffer and shorter the muscle grows. As that happens, the muscle also loses its ability to absorb the strain of repetitive athletic motions, making it far more susceptible to pulls and tears. The nagging minor injuries that start to show up every so often in our 40s and gradually become annoyingly familiar are more the result of decreasing flexibility than of increasing years. An 8,000-yard workout might leave a 20-year-old's muscles limber and pliant. At 40, swimming a third of that distance could tighten tissue enough to trigger an injury.

But even if an unstretched muscle doesn't get hurt, it can still get in your way. Tight muscles don't work as well as stretched ones, and that means your swimming suffers. Any muscle not periodically stretched back to its full length gradually accepts its contracted state as normal, and you lose range of motion in that joint. Less motion for the joint generally means less motion for you, and that also applies while you're swimming.

Though athletes, when they bother to stretch at all, invariably treat it as a preworkout warmup, you should invest some time on muscle flexibility before *and* after your practice. Stretching before you swim helps prevent muscle soreness. Stretching afterward relieves any you might have gotten despite stretching before. It also helps speed the removal of waste products and the supply of nutrients to repair and restore the muscle for future work.

Always precede preworkout limbering-up exercises with a brief, gentle warmup since warm muscles are more supple and responsive.

"No pain, no gain" does not apply here. Stretch just to the point at which pain is barely starting, then back off slightly. Not only is hurting yourself not a good idea, but pain causes muscles to contract. Not the effect you were looking for. Breathe normally through a stretch, and usually after 30 seconds or so you'll feel the muscle relax a little. That's your cue. Immediately go a little farther to take up the slack, but stay away from the bouncing movements of so-called "ballistic" stretching. They can actually tighten you right back up again.

The ideal duration of each stretch is 30 seconds to a minute, since it takes that long for the muscle to adjust fully. But not many people have the patience. If that describes you, hold the stretch instead for maybe 10 to 12 seconds, then relax briefly, and repeat four to five times. And *never* have a partner push you into a more-stretched position. That's just asking for an injury.

Relax! (Some Swim-Specific Stretches)

Besides a general flexibility once-over, I recommend a couple of specific exercises that focus on swimming's trouble spots, the muscles most likely to get dangerously tight as you stroke. Do two reps of each, 10 to 30 seconds per rep, before and again after your practice.

1. The Muscles Underneath the Shoulder: Put both arms overhead in the streamlined position, then lean first to the left side as far as possible, then to the right. You should feel the pull all the way down your side.

2. The Muscles in Front of the Shoulder: Put both arms behind your back, fingers interlaced, and slowly, steadily raise your arms upward behind you as far as possible.

3. *The Muscles in Back of the Shoulder:* Put one arm across your body, shoulder under your chin with hand, forearm, and upper arm parallel to ground. Without turning your body, use your other hand to pull the arm as close to your chest as possible.

Fine. But what about stretches for the rest of your body? You certainly don't need me to suggest any, since routines are out there by the hundreds in one exercise book after another.

Unfortunately, in most cases they're typical maintenance work, about as exciting to do as changing the oil in your car. So I do have a recommendation, because that's just how bored I felt when I started looking around for a stretching plan that would be more fun to do—and preferably more effective—than the usual humdrum "Big Five" or "Essential Six" that you see over and over in all the exercise books. It was worth the search. And I can now recommend to you an excellent flexibility builder that's both effective and appealing: Yoga. After trying practically every stretching trick in the book, I found that Yoga exercises (or postures, as they're properly called) are far more exciting than plain stretching, do more good, and do more to balance your body. All I can say is, besides swimming, Yoga is the only physical activity I'm determined to do for the rest of my life. It makes me feel better in and out of the pool.

But Yoga is a little like artistic painting. You can learn enough to do an acceptable job quickly, or you can study it for the rest of your life with no end in sight. And there are practically as many styles in the one discipline as in the other. I certainly couldn't begin to explain it to you here. But I can tell you that one of the best-known Yoga programs for athletes, and deservedly so, is Beryl Bender Birch's Power Yoga, the official Yoga program of the New York Road Runners Club, which she teaches around the country. Birch's *Power Yoga* (Simon & Schuster) might tell you more than you really need to know, but it does so engagingly and entertainingly. And you will end up getting a lot more out of your limbering-up time.

4. *Get Strong: A Healthy Shoulder Takes 10 Minutes.* To most athletes who use their arms over their heads—like pitchers and swimmers—shoulder injury and rotator cuff injury mean practically the same thing. The rotator cuff is actually a team of four little muscles that hold your arm bone (the golf ball, remember) onto its shoulder socket (the tee). And given the frequency with which weak or overused rotator cuff muscles cause trouble, it's worth stopping the problem before it starts. Ten minutes a day spent on the exercises below, as recommended by sports medicine specialist Lewis G. Maharam, M.D., FACSM, who is Medical Director of the Metropolitan Athletics Congress in New York City, can give you good insurance against shoulder pain. Do each once or twice a day in the order outlined below, one arm at a time, for 50 repetitions, with a three- to five-pound dumbbell. Make sure you do 50 reps, even if you must reduce the weight. And it's important to lower the weight slowly in all exercises.

Biceps Curls: Do them standing and to full extension.

Reverse Biceps Curls: Same as above, but turn hand in opposite direction (palm down).

Front Lift: Arm straight down, palm forward, raise up until parallel to floor, then lower slowly.

Reverse Front Lift: Same as above but start with palm facing back.

Out to Side: Same as above but start with palm facing in and lift out to side.

Adduction: Bend forward at waist, arm hanging straight down and palm facing in. Raise arm across body until inside of forearm crosses chest. Lower slowly to starting point.

Abduction: Same as above, but raise arm out to side parallel to floor, then lower slowly.

Side Lift: Lying on your side, upper arm against your body (elbow lying on rib cage), arm in handshake position, rotate arm so forearm points to ceiling, then lower slowly.

Wing Lift: Lie on your side, holding your top elbow against your ribs, bent to 90 degrees. Slowly raise the weight until elbow points to ceiling, then lower it slowly.

Reverse Wing Lift: Lie on your back, upper arm close to your side, forearm on floor with palm up, elbow at 90-degree angle. Rotate forearm until weight points to the ceiling, then lower it slowly.

Seems like a lot of bother? Maybe, until you realize that it can take up to 16 weeks for rotator cuff problems to heal. It's the knowing swimmer who strengthens those muscles *before* trouble starts.

Thanks to the gentleness of swimming's weightless and fluid motion, it doesn't take much to stay pain free. Warm up, stretch, swim smoothly, warm down, and stay strong. Since the proverbial ounce of prevention now will do the job, there's no reason to put yourself through the pound of cure later.

Chapter 17

Your Friends Are Waiting
("Whom Can I Swim With? And Where?")

Though long-distance running is supposedly the sport of loneliness—at least the movie title tells us so—a good case could also be made for swimming. Think about it. You can't hear a thing except your own breathing, conversation is out of the question, and the view is pretty much limited to green water and black lines. Hard to imagine a more solitary way to work out.

Or a more friendly one, either. Perhaps it's a reaction to that private little cocoon we do all our laps in, but swimmers as a group are wonderfully congenial. And that's a good thing, because it's far easier to become truly proficient as a member of a group than alone. Thanks to the extensive network of local, regional, and national groups, nearly anyone can.

Even if you're not a joiner, you'll want to rethink a purely solo-workout schedule. I swim alone most of the time too, but when I can practice with friends, I always swim faster and I always enjoy it more. Faster because even friendly competition gives you a push—it's just good, healthy instinct to race a little when someone's in the lane next to yours. More enjoyable because no matter how soothing solo workouts can be, you can't tell yourself new jokes, cheer yourself on, pat yourself on the back for a personal best, or laugh off a disappointing finishing time. That takes lane-mates. And though joining U.S. Masters Swimming is the most powerful tool for finding them, there are other good ways too. Whatever you do, please follow through on at least one of the following suggestions. As your Total Immersion skills grow, you're going to enjoy swimming more and more—probably for a long time to come. You'll grow faster and enjoy the journey more with company.

Swimming With Friends/Finding Friends to Swim With

1. *The Buddy System:* Find a compatible training partner and make a pact to meet at the pool one or more times a week. Not only will you feel more obliged to keep the appointment and end up swimming more regularly, you'll both swim better with company.

You'll probably soon find you weren't alone looking for training mates, as your little band grows. One winter I decided I needed the push of meeting a couple of friends to work out at 6:30 each morning. Frequently, our "workout circle" grew by five or six people as other stray predawn exercisers asked if they too could join up. Casual team formation like this is the most convenient and flexible way to gain the benefits of swimming with other people. You can even get some impromptu coaching, since workout-mates are always happy to watch you stroke or drill. Just tell them what you're practicing and what to look for, preferably underwater through goggles.

2. *Joining U.S. Masters Swimming:* Don't be put off by the word "Masters." It doesn't mean what you may think, as I'll explain in a moment.

A Masters team, in fact, is probably the best place to swim with friends of all abilities and make new ones. You'll also have a coach to plan your workouts and help you improve your stroke, though there's a wide range of professionalism, energy, and attention levels among Masters coaches. Some seem to have a gift for making every practice better than the one before. Others are little more than lifeguards. You won't know until you try, though asking members before you join can usually produce reliable opinions. You do lose some flexibility in

scheduling your swim with a Masters group, but you can always practice with the team when it's convenient and on your own when
it's not.

Above all, know that "Masters" is not a code word for "serious"
and "elite." A tiny percentage of Masters swimmers fit that description, but most probably swim just like you do—or they did until they
joined a Masters team and jump-started their progress.

Before 1972, there wasn't much a postcollegiate swimmer could do
but retire. I know I did. Adults swim competitively? Whoever heard
of such a thing? Then Ransom Arthur, a U.S. Navy medical officer,
decided people needed a rewarding way to stay fit, and he essentially
launched the Masters (adult) swimming movement. At first, U.S. Masters Swimming simply tried to provide organized competitions for
adults, but the fitness swimming movement was gaining momentum
so fast that the new group could hardly stop there. Today, in fact, only
a third of the more than 30,000 Masters members compete. Most join
with no intention of ever racing. They're strictly fitness and recre-
ational swimmers who love the sport, want to meet other people who
do too, and are looking for coaching to help them along.

It's a personal and personable organization. For though U.S. Masters Swimming is the national administrative body, the grassroots
foundation—all most swimmers ever see anyway—are the 50 Local
Masters Swim Committees (LMSCs) which oversee Masters swimming groups in their areas. The LMSCs handle registration, organize
and sanction meets, maintain regular communications with their
members, and often have social activities as well. The national office
coordinates among the LMSCs, organizes National and Postal meets
(see "Mail-in Meets: The Thirty-two-Cent Swimming Test," pg. 245),
and provides insurance for all members.

What you actually join is the Local Masters Swim Committee, from

Your Friends Are Waiting — — — — — — — — — —

which you get a monthly newsletter with swim tips, event schedules, and results of local meets. You'll also receive insurance coverage during events if you do decide to race, and a subscription to *Swim,* the national organization's bimonthly magazine for adult fitness swimmers. Not bad for annual dues of $20 to $25. (For more information on U.S. Masters Swimming, call Executive Secretary Dorothy Donnelly at (508)886-6631. She'll put you in touch with the registrar for your area's LMSC, who can in turn tell you where to find a coached group or at least places where you can swim laps on your own.)

Masters groups are like swimmers themselves: They run the gamut from loose and informal to highly structured and organized. Most groups include swimmers of both kinds and many in between, all working out happily under the same roof. In one or two lanes, you'll find former competitive swimmers who train intensely, whether for meets or for fitness. In the intermediate lanes, there are swimmers who came to the sport a little later, and who suit up for the occasional Masters meet (plus triathletes who aren't going crazy because they have two other sports to put their energies into). And in the rest, fitness swimmers who joined mainly for coaching pointers and camaraderie. If your skills are sound (i.e., you can consistently swim an average of 20 strokes per length), a team environment will push you along far faster.

Larger teams are usually better organized, with more practices and better coaching, but you may not get much attention. Smaller groups may offer fewer practices and less experienced coaches, but you may get lots of one-on-one advice. And they all have one thing in common —a life outside the pool. Nearly all teams sponsor social activities to a greater or lesser degree. Despite all that, you'll probably choose the same way most of us do: Find the group that offers the most convenient practice location and schedule, and stick with it.

"What's Going On Here?"
(Rules of the Road in the pool)

Pools are not like parks. You can't just throw a bunch of athletes in and let them work out any old way they please. Space is too tight, lanes are too confining. So swimmers observe an unspoken but certainly not unofficial etiquette that is not only polite but practical, fitting in as many people as possible, doing the workouts they need safely, smoothly, and without collisions.

The sooner you know the rules, the better you'll fit in wherever you find yourself swimming. Fortunately, just like the rules of the road for cars, the conventions in pools are pretty similar all over the U.S., which means you should be able to fit in smoothly anywhere. But just to be sure, check with the lifeguard at any unfamiliar pool. They may have invented something new there.

1. Picking Your Lane: In a busy pool, specific lanes are usually reserved for faster, moderate, and slower-speed swimmers and are often identified by signs on the wall, deck, or starting block. Of course, those speed terms are relative. "Fast" could mean 1:15 per 100 yards in one pool, 1:45 in another. So your best bet is to eyeball each lane and pick the one that looks best for you. Worry about labels some other time.

If no directions are posted, then it's kind of frontier justice: Possession is nine-tenths of the law. Whoever's already there

continued

sets the lane's pace. If you're faster than the pace-setters, back off. Today might be a good time to work on your stroke instead of your speed.

You'll certainly be swimming more slowly during the first five or ten minutes as you warm up, so you may want to start in a slower lane, then switch to a faster one later. Or, if you've been swimming for awhile and decide to do a kicking set which will slow you down, it makes sense to switch lanes.

2. Getting In: Rule one: no diving. Ever. It's not safe, and even if you happen to think it is, the pool's insurance company disagrees. Lower yourself down gently, feet first, anywhere lap swimming is going on.

Then, don't just barge in. You'll be sharing tight space with strangers, and pushing off whenever you feel like it is no way to show goodwill and cooperation. If someone is obviously in the middle of a long swim and won't be stopping any time soon, slip into the pool and stand to the side of the lane for a minute or so, allowing them to see you before you start. And never push off immediately in front of or behind someone else. Allow at least five or ten seconds of cushion either way.

3. Navigating: If there's just one other swimmer in the lane, you two can split it if you want, each taking a side. It's first-come, first-served, so ask as you're getting in whether your lane-mate would prefer to circle or split. With three or more, there's obviously no choice but to circle. So if you'll be the third and the first two are splitting, slip in, stand to one side until they both notice you, and ask if they'd mind switching to a circle pattern.

Circling is nearly always counterclockwise. Think of the line on the bottom as the highway divider and stay to the right, as close to the lane rope as possible.

4. *Passing*: Sometimes, even with everyone in a lane supposedly moving along at the same clip, you'll come steaming up on someone's soles. To pass, tap him on the feet *only once* during the lap. When you reach the next wall, he'll move right and you'll pass on the left. If you are the ''passee,'' of course, yield by moving to the right at the next wall.

Don't be stubborn when you're doing intervals. It's everyone's pool, and to make that work you may have to be flexible enough to adjust your timing up or down to give other swimmers some space. Slower swimmer coming in toward the end of your interval countdown? Shave your rest a little and leave before she gets there, instead of pushing off the instant she goes by and immediately having to pass. If a faster swimmer's coming in, extend your interval a few seconds so you push off behind him, rather than getting in his way.

Common sense and awareness will get you everywhere. If a swimmer behind you is coming up fast enough to catch you on the next length, don't even wait until she taps your feet. Stop at the next wall and let her by. Good manners are always appreciated. And almost always reciprocated.

5. *Resting*: To take a breather, squeeze into the right-side corner (your right as you swim toward the wall). To take a long breather, more than a couple of minutes, sit on the deck completely out of the way.

continued

Your Friends Are Waiting — — — — — — — — — —

So much for the actual swimming part. On the deck: 1. Never loiter in front of the pace clock. After all, people can't read through you; and 2. Don't borrow the equipment sitting at the end of the lane without asking, even if it looks like it's not being used.

Masters Swim Meets: You Can't Lose

These days I'm actually surprised when a new swimmer even mentions wanting to enter a Masters meet or open-water race someday. New runners seem ready to fill out their first road race application the minute their Nikes are broken in. What is it about swim meets that makes lap swimmers—even those who have been at it for decades— think the contests are just for experts? If runners were such pessimists, every 10K race would be over in a blink, maybe under 40 minutes. No one who took longer would bother showing up.

Swimmers don't know what they're missing. After you've been practicing your Total Immersion drills for awhile and your stroke has begun to feel smoother, easier, and faster, the best way to test your progress is swimming in a Masters meet.

"But I'm not in it for the medals," you say. Good. Neither are most other Masters. The best way to once and for all explode the myth that Masters meets are for bloodthirsty award hounds is to watch one. Grassroots pastime or national championship, you'll see competitors of all ages who probably wouldn't stand out in any YMCA lap session. True, the whiz kids might knock off 100 yards of freestyle in 45 seconds, but others will take three minutes . . . and they'll get hearty applause for a job well done.

What most astonishes former college swimmers like me, people who remember meets as pressure-cooker contests of grim determination, is the relaxed, folksy feeling at Masters meets. Having a good time comes first, turning in a good time comes second. Competition is against the clock, not against each other.

Most people don't talk about why they won't race. The ones who do are concerned about lacking the following three skills. I hope these people don't wait until they've acquired them, because you don't need a single one:

1. You Must Execute a Racing Start Off a High Platform. No you mustn't. Masters swimmers are free to start their races in the water—and often do, simply because they feel more comfortable that way.

2. You Have to Be Able to Do Racing Flip Turns. Wrong again. The easily learned open turn is common at Masters meets. I've seen swimmers win national titles with them.

3. You'll be Racing Against Former Collegiate Stars. Nonsense. First, only a third of the swimmers at Masters meets have had any previous competitive swimming experience. Second, if you're new to this, you'll be swimming with other new swimmers anyway since heats are seeded by estimated time. Many meets even offer novice-only races, restricted to those who have never swum the event competitively. You could be a medalist your first time out.

It generally works this way. At meets, men and women are divided into five-year age groups for scoring purposes, beginning with 19 to 24 and continuing up to 100-plus. But heats are normally seeded according to time, with no regard for age or sex. A 24-year-old woman could be swimming next to a 62-year-old man if their times are expected to be similar.

In fact, you're ready for a Masters meet if you can swim two lengths of a 25-yard pool in good form (50 yards is the minimum distance in Masters meets). Most people can finish off a 50-yard race in 30 seconds to a minute. Freestyle and backstroke are the least technical events. Forget breaststroke and butterfly for now. Legal breaststroke requires a froglike kick that feels ungainly to many novices and, as for butterfly, even two lengths is a challenge for anyone.

And when Masters say freestyle, they mean *freestyle*. As in free to choose any style you like. Most of us use the so-called crawl because it's generally fastest, but you're the boss. In 1992, I watched two 90-something gentlemen race neck-and-neck in a 200-meter freestyle contest in the Masters World Championships. Both were using an elementary backstroke, perfectly legal under the rules.

Finally, pick any event distance you want—right up to the longest, which is the 1,500-meter freestyle, just this side of a mile—so long as you can complete the race without standing up or holding onto lane lines. Masters National and even World Championships are all-comers meets, with all competitors guaranteed the right to swim in three events without meeting any qualifying times. Local, state, and even regional meets never require qualifying times for entry to any number of events.

Don't mistakenly think the best ways to ease into swim racing are the short 50-or 100-yard events because they're over fast and how bad can you look? Shorter races take more skill, power, and speed to avoid being left way behind. You're better off going maybe 500 yards, which also gives you time to work on things you've been practicing, like form and pace. Besides, it will feel more like your practice swimming than the breakneck speed of a short sprint.

You needn't be in superb shape to handle 500 yards either. Remember our rule of 70: 70 percent of your swim performance comes from your stroke mechanics and only 30 percent from fitness. Once you can swim for about eight minutes nonstop in a practice, you probably have a 500-yard event inside.

Mail-in Meets: The Thirty-two-Cent Swimming Test

Want a race all your own? No spectators, no specific starting time, no noise, no pressure?

Postal meets (you just mail in your results and officials handle the scoring) are as no-pressure as they get. Betty Barry of Victor, New York, has directed a postal meet called the 2000 Fitness Challenge for a couple of years, and says a third of her entrants are people who have never been in any kind of organized swimming event before. "One woman sent me a note with her entry that said, 'I don't want to get up on the blocks; I don't want to have to race anybody; I'm so happy that you've given me the opportunity to do something meaningful by myself in my own pool.'"

Like a chess match played by mail, you never meet your rivals face to face in a postal event. Swim in whatever pool suits you, at your own convenience, the only required spectator being a lap counter/timer of your choice. When you're done, write your result on the entry form, have your witness sign it, and mail it to the tabulator. A couple of weeks later, you're notified how you placed against everyone else who did the same thing. It's as private and civilized as an unpublished phone number.

And more varied than a "real" meet. Short events, long events, events just for kicking with fins, one for the maximum distance swum in one hour, another for the grand total of your

continued

February yardage. Awards are always tabulated by sex and five-year age group, as they are in regular Masters meets.

Postal events can juice up your training with the motivation that can come only from entering a race. And they're real money-savers. You can compare yourself to other swimmers your age from all over the country without ever having to buy a plane ticket.

(U.S. Masters Swimming Executive Secretary Dorothy Donnelly at (508)886-6631 can provide a schedule of postal events.)

No Lanes, No Lights—The Wide-Open-Water Swim

Open-water swims are not nearly as "clubby" as Masters meets, but they're just as relaxing in their own way. And it's for the same reasons that road races are so much more popular than track meets among runners—freedom of the "open road" and the happy anonymity of competing in a field of hundreds.

Just as thousands of foot-powered athletes would never consider the military regimentation of a track meet, open-water competitions draw swimmers who never race in a pool. Without the intimidation of timers standing watchfully around the deck, rivals challenging from neighboring starting blocks, and bleachers full of curious fans peering at the water—maybe even at you—open-water events are as matter-of-fact as a weekend 10K. Proof: though U.S. Masters Swimming has some 30,000 registered members, only a third enter meets, as we said earlier. Yet 50,000 people swim in open-water races connected with triathlons each year, and thousands more crowd the shorelines at open-water swims. Who needs the coddled precision of lanes? For the price of an occasional foot in the face or elbow in the ear from one of the other unguided bodies, you have freedom.

So why is it many swimmers never venture out of the pool to explore the exhilaration of swimming in lakes, rivers, and oceans? Timidity. Swimming without a line to guide you, a bottom you can see, and a wall nearby for comfort? Buoys you have to find so you don't get lost, perhaps surf to fight, and who knows what else in the water out there besides swimmers? No, thanks.

All manageable risks, and clearly worth the managing when you finally plunge in off the beach and your body remembers that before chlorine, before filters and pumps, even before electric lights, this is how we swam. There may be no wall to touch for security, but there's no wall hemming you in either.

Obviously, without the customary safety net of lifeguards, bottoms to stand on, and walls or lane markers to hold onto, you've got to ready a safety net of your own. Here's how to put it in place:

Feeling at Home at Sea: Strategies

Back at the Pool:

You'll adapt to open-water conditions much faster if you first sharpen a couple of skills in the pool.

1. Practice bilateral breathing. You can't be certain of getting air on your more comfortable side during an open-water race. Wind and waves may be against you and your landmarks may be on your "other" side, so you need to be able to roll your head either way at any time.

2. Practice swimming and looking up and forward two to three times per pool length. Visualize what you're looking for *before* you lift your head. This will teach you to spot your landmarks right away, holding onto your rhythm and balance as you do.

3. Swim some short repeats, perhaps 25 or 50 yards, head up or "Tarzan-style," staying focused on a poolside landmark. In a race, you're going to have to poke your head out of the water until you find what you're looking for. This will acquaint you with stroke adjustments you might make while doing so.

4. Swim several 25-yard repeats with your eyes closed to test your ability to swim straight when the water's murky and there's nothing to guide on. Do this slowly in case you run into a lane line, and wait until you have a lane to yourself unless you enjoy getting a reputation as an unguided torpedo. Count strokes, and open your eyes when you calculate you're still four short of the wall. No accidents please. This will teach you to swim straight without a lane line for guidance.

Before the Race:

1. Obviously you want to do some swimming in a lake or the ocean first. You'll get used to the absence of convenient guides like lane lines and will learn to navigate instinctively using on-shore landmarks. *Safety first:* Swim with an experienced partner or in a group, or with an escort canoe or kayak. Be careful in cold water and stay close to shore. Hypothermia (lowered body temperature) can impair your coordination and cloud your judgment. A wetsuit, if you have one, will be good insulation.

INSIDE MARKE

Inside Triathlon CLASSIFIEDS WORK! $35 for the first 25 words, $1 for each additional word. Each consecutive repeat insertion of the same ad is 25% off the original price, AND/OR you may run the same ad in the next issue of VeloNews for a 25% discount. You get an extra 48,000 readers with your ad in VeloNews! Prepayment required. Send ad and payment (check or Visa/Master Card) to Inside Triathlon Classifieds, 1830 N 55th St, Boulder, CO 80301, or fax your ad with your credit card information: 303/444-6788. Bike ads are sorted and listed by size of bike, smallest to largest. Please include state in your ad copy. DEADLINES: November 2 for January issue; November 30 for February issue; December 28 for March issue. Ads must be received by 12 noon Mountain Time.

PARTS FOR SALE

WHEELS, PARTS, ACCESSORIES: unbeatable prices. Wheelsets starting at $69.95/pr. Our prices make cycling more affordable. Price list available. L. Bico, Box 29, Corunna, MI 48817. 517/743-5987.

BICYCLES FOR SALE

Subaru Presents: The 10TH ANNUAL VELOSWAP & EXPO — the World's Largest Consumer Cycling Show & Swap Meet. Saturday, October 24th, 1998, 9 a.m. to 5 p.m. at the National Western Complex in Denver, Colorado. Produced by the staffs of VeloNews and Inside Triathlon magazines. For more information, call the VeloSwap Hotline 303/440-0601 ext. 222, or see our web-site: www.velonews.com/swap

SPECIALIZED M2 frames, road and mountain; $299. Bolle sunglasses, 50% off. PINARELLO Cross frame and fork; $599. KESTREL bike blowout; call for price. The Pedaler, phone: 510/222-3420, fax: 510/222-6168 (CA), www.theped.com, e-mail: help@theped.com

LITESPEED Titanium, any model/size, framesets, complete bicycles, AFFORDABLE PRICES. Spinergy, Mavic wheelsets; $499.90. Campy, Shimano gruppos. Bicycle Doctor, 8551 West Gardner, Bloomington, IN 812/825-5050.

Medium size LOTUS Road frame/fork, includes hs, bb, extra dropout set and extra seat post assembly, black carbon w/yellow decals, exc cond, never crashed; $3250. Paris Roubaix road Rock Shox; $200. Ryan 405/359-2952. (OK)

FOR SALE OTHER

INSIDE TRIATHLON CASES provide an easy way to organize & store your issues for future reference. Durable leather-like material, hot-stamped in gold, these forest green cases are an attractive addition to your home library. Price: one for $8.95; three for $24.95; six for $45.95. Add $1.50 per case for postage and handling. Outside Continental US (including AK & HI) add $3.50 per case (US funds only). Order from: Inside Triathlon, Jesse Jones Industries, Dept 98 IT, 499 E Erie Ave, Philadelphia, PA 19134. Include your name, address (no PO boxes please) and payment with your order. PA residents add 7% sales tax. Allow 4 to 6 weeks for delivery. Credit card orders: Amex, Visa, MasterCard, Diners Club accepted. Send card name, number, exp date, or call toll-free 24 hours a day 800/825-6690. Satisfaction guaranteed.

FOR SALE OTHER

"TRIATHLETE - Swim Bike Run" license plate frames! $7.50 ea 2/$10 + $2.50 s&h. Free brochure. Sport Frames, PO Box 11 , Tacoma, WA 98411. 206/588-3049.

See AMERICA BY BICYCLE fast. Great Coast to Coast training ride. Los Angeles to Boston, 3,300 miles - 32 days (average mileage 110 per day). Fully supported, hotel lodging, meals, SAG & Mechanic. America by Bicycle, P.O. Box 805-I, Atkinson, NH 03811. http://www.abbike.com. 1-888-797-7057.

HELP WANTED

LEARN ABOUT THE PUBLISHING AND TRIATHLON INDUSTRIES FROM THE INSIDE. Inside Communications, publisher of VeloNews, Inside Triathlon and VeloBusiness, seeks interns for its editorial, advertising sales, photo, interactive and circulation/marketing departments. 12 week commitment (15-20 hours per week) minimum requirement. Positions are unpaid. For information, send resume and cover letter to: Inside Triathlon Interns, Attn: Hilarie, 1830 N 55th St, Boulder, CO 80301. E-mail hporter@7dogs.com. No phone calls, please.

Inside Communications, publisher of VeloNews, Inside Triathlon and

APPAREL

EYEWEAR

On Race Day:

1. If you can't swim out and check the course itself, at least study a map. Picture how important landmarks—notably the finish line—will look from the water. Check with the lifeguards for water temperature, prevailing currents, and, if it's an ocean race, surf conditions.

2. Count how many buoys you have to pass or turn on, and on which side you need to pass them. Check bottom contours for the areas where you'll be entering and leaving the water. How far can you run and "porpoise," and where will you need to start swimming?

3. If wetsuits are allowed in the race, wear one. You'll swim about 5 percent faster without working any harder for it.

During the Race:

1. Open-water races usually begin with a mass(-confusion) start. Stay off to the side, even if you have to swim a slightly longer course to the first buoy. You'll be out of the middle of the pack, where a collision with a stray arm or leg could ruin your rhythm, knock your goggles off, or, in rare cases, do some real damage.

2. Look for someone slightly faster than you are to draft behind. Drafting will let you swim a little faster with no more exertion, not to mention letting you get away with lifting your head for navigation much less often. You can just keep your face in the water and follow the pack. You can, that is, if your draftee knows where he's going.

3. You may need to adjust your stroke for ocean swimming. Don't worry. Methodical pool swimmers often find waves upset their rhythm, so don't fight it. Just feel the swells and roll with them. A high-elbow recovery is also essential in choppy water. And since you're more buoyant in salt water than fresh, you can lay off the kick

and just focus on your speed-enhancing front-quadrant swimming and the rhythmic rolling of your hips for power.

4. If it's a triathlon swim, don't sprint at the end. Just hold your pace, keep your heart rate low, and save your energy for the bike and run. As you near shore, swim just until your hands touch bottom, then stand and begin running to shore with a high-knee gait.

Taking It All on the Road

Well, we're almost done. By now, I hope you're looking at swimming in a whole new way—as a sport of finely honed skill, not brute strength; a sport where power flows effortlessly from the core of your body to limbs that have learned to wring every inch of good out of it; and a sport where you're never as good as you're going to get because the human nervous system continues to be a wonderful learning machine long after the body's physical peak is reached.

What a shame it would be if you had to leave all this behind every time you left home. But you don't. Most successful swimmers eventually master one last skill: knowing how to find places to work out, from one end of the country to the other, whether it's a one-day conference that sends you out of town or a six-month sabbatical.

If you're a member of U.S. Masters Swimming, of course, finding friendly faces to work out with is probably just a phone call away (see Where to Go for What). If not, or if there's no Masters group within striking distance of your destination and you just need a suitable body of water, you'll need to do a little additional research. In 1990, for example, I spent eight days driving from New York to San Diego, swimming every single day of the trip. I was lucky. With coaching friends all over the country, it was easy to find pools and arrange for swim time.

Today, it's common for dedicated swimmers who travel regularly to go to great lengths to maintain their swim schedule on the road, finding the hotels in each city they visit that offer the best lap pools or, failing that, at least locating a convenient pool that permits daily passes. It's so common, in fact, that someone has finally done all the research for you. If you are or aspire to be one of these creatures of healthy habit, you'll be happy to know that all the information you need has now been compiled into an unassuming little book called *Swimmer's Guide: Directory of Pools for Fitness Swimmers,* which lists over 3,000 year-round pools in hotels, health clubs, schools, and municipal facilities in 1,700 U.S. cities. You'd like names, addresses, phone numbers, admission fees, schedules, pool lengths and water temperatures? You got 'em. For information on obtaining your own copy, call my Total Immersion office at (800)609–7946.

Once you start swimming better than you ever thought you could, you'll never want to stop, even briefly. And frankly, nothing could make me happier.

Happy laps!

AFTERWORD

"You now have the power in your hands," as they say to the hero in science fiction movies. "But you must use it only for good."

I would like to leave you with the same thought about Total Immersion swimming. As effective as I know this program can be in guiding your swimming progress, don't let that obscure the reason for swimming in the first place—your body loves being in the water.

Because balanced bodies, weightless arms, and pace clocks aside, this is really all about having fun.

One of the most rewarding letters I've ever received from a Total Immersion workshop alumnus came from Volker Winkler, a Tennessee physician and triathlete. "As a result of your coaching," he wrote, "I've improved my 1,500-meter time by two minutes, which is all I had hoped for. But something far more important, and unexpected, happened as well. I used to just tolerate swimming as a necessity for triathlon. Yet after taking your course I now look forward to and *enjoy* my swims. Since I'll be swimming for much longer than I'll be doing triathlons, that is a great gift."

Unless you're a lifeguard or a castaway, you probably don't *have* to swim. It's not a job, it's recreation. As sports psychologist and highly ranked Masters swimmer Keith Bell, Ph.D., wrote: "I find it strange that people 'play' golf, 'play' tennis, and 'play' volleyball; but when they swim they 'work out.' I never work out. I 'play' swimming. I play intensely, but it is play. Beats the heck out of working out."

Children are wiser about such matters. Like most of us, I learned to "play" swimming when I was very young. In fact, I played at it all afternoon, every day, all summer long, simply enjoying the freedom of movement and weightlessness that being in the water offers. But as we grow up, things are suddenly supposed to have results. In my teens I became a competitive swimmer, which meant the point of the sport was now getting from here to there as fast as I could, preferably faster than anybody else. I had begun the descent into the seriousness of the goal-oriented adult: I'd forgotten how to play.

And the better I got at working out—at giving it everything I had—the less I enjoyed the sport. In college, swimming faster than ever, I couldn't wait to graduate and quit. It just hurt too much, and for what?

Twenty-five years later I'm competing once again, and even doing some intense training beforehand. But it's different—and better—now. I've found my way back to the *swimming* part of competitive swimming, letting the touch of the water support me, gliding forward with as little effort as possible and even less fuss. I have luckily reconnected with the joy of swimming, and I look forward to doing it for the rest of my life.

Whatever you do, please don't make swimming well a business when it should be a pleasure. That's not what this program is about. Every Total Immersion lesson is a chance to develop the sensual pleasures of swimming well, just as much as it's a lesson in correct form. In fact, at the end of every workshop, as campers are gathering their things to leave, I call them together for a send-off message: "Please. Make your swimming *fun*. Pay attention to how it feels. Enjoy the growing sensation of effortless speed. That's what the tools you've acquired here are for."

Sensory skill practice feels good. Stroke counting and swimming golf turn a goal into a game. Going from drill to drill keeps your body fresh and your mind alert. And up on deck, there are fellow swimmers and future friends waiting to hear why you look like you're enjoying it so much.

Learning to swim well is good, and worthwhile, and one of the best gifts you can give yourself. It's the only sport I can do better at 45 than I could at 15. The fun is back. And I'm not letting it get away again. Don't you, either.

APPENDIX
THE TOTAL IMMERSION PRACTICES

Once you understand that swimming is a technique sport, not a power sport, you also understand that *any* drill work will do more for you than just swimming lap after lap ever could. But chances are, you also now want to make the most of your Total Immersion program time. How much stroke practice, how much sensory skill work, and how much "real" swimming should you do for the best results? And what's the best way to do them?

Here are a dozen-and-a-half answers, 18 sample practices that show you how to take the lessons of the Total Immersion program and put them into an efficient, effective training format. Remember, they are just examples to get you started. Eventually, as your body learns what "right swimming" should feel like, you'll know all by yourself what to concentrate on and how much work you need. Meantime, these practices will give you some experience in designing your own sessions, sessions that will keep you tightly focused on improving stroke mechanics (70 percent of your performance, remember!) while staying fit.

The six **Skill-Builder** practices are just that: a step-by-step series of workouts that will gradually introduce your body to your new, Total Immersion swim stroke. Stay with each one until you're comfortable with it, then move on to the next. But by all means go back for a "refresher" to an earlier practice whenever you think you need it.

The six **Intermediate** practices step up the pace. In these, you spend less time building skills and more time actually swimming with them—checking your progress every step of the way and making Total

Immersion swimming feel more and more natural and instinctive for your body. The centerpiece of several of the practices is a set that challenges you to hang on to your good stroke mechanics as things gradually get tougher—more distance, less rest, or more speed (sometimes all at once!). This main set is always supplemented by others that accomplish much the same thing but don't push you as hard.

And of course the six **Veteran** practices speak for themselves. When you're ready for the ultimate in both fitness and fluid swimming, you're ready for these.

New swimmers especially will probably look at all the abbreviations and wonder if this is swim practice or an algebra class. Don't worry—it's not complicated at all, and it's worth getting used to the shorthand and the structure. Remember: *The biggest difference between Total Immersion practices and conventional workouts is that every length of every Total Immersion set has a purpose.* Eventually you'll be able to decide for yourself what that purpose should be for that particular day, which is why the samples offer lots of variety—variety that will not only keep the whole process interesting but help you actually learn more and learn faster.

By "cutting and pasting" sets from one or more practices into other practices, you can design an almost limitless number of Total Immersion sessions for yourself. Feel free to modify sets for greater or lesser difficulty by increasing or decreasing the number of repeats or rounds in a set, or by increasing or reducing the distance of repeats or the suggested rest interval.

Here we go. First, the shorthand you'll need to be comfortable with:

Definitions and Abbreviations

Drill Shorthand: *See Chapter 8 for Complete Drill Explanations.*

RA: Single arm with the right arm
LA: Same with the left arm
CU: Catchup, alternating single arm
S&G-3: Slide & glide—3-count pauses in each position
ASG: Advanced slide & glide

SSP Shorthand: *See Chapter 7 for Complete Sensory Skill Practice Explanations.*

DH: Swim downhill
RW: Reach for the far wall
WA: Swim with a weightless arm
HS: Hand-swapping or semicatchup
BB: Point your belly button at sidewalls
HR: Concentrate on developing hip rhythm

Miscellaneous:

@ RI: Designates the rest interval in minutes and seconds to be taken after completing one swim and before beginning the next
s/l: Strokes per length ("-1 s/l" indicates one less s/l than your normal)
Golf: Swimming golf. Add your s/l to time in seconds to get your score (see Chapter 7)
Pace: Swim at what feels like race pace for your best race distance
EZ: Swim at easy or very relaxed pace
Build: Increase speed throughout a swim. Easy at the beginning, finish at a faster pace

Appendix — — — — — — — — — —

Descend: Swim faster on each successive repeat in a set. Example: "4 x 50 descend" could mean #1 = :43, #2 = :42, #3 = :41, #4 = :40.

Note: #1 in each practice is a uniform 300-yard warmup of "mixed" strokes. Swim easily and gently, using a different stroke or drill (your choice) each length. You can use the same stroke or drill more than once, but not on consecutive lengths.

Skill-Builder Practices

These are pure, relaxed, "learning sessions," sessions that are the bridge from ordinary fitness swimming (just laps) to skilled and ulti-mately organized and challenging workouts.

Skill-Builder 1: Perfectly Balanced

1. Warmup (see note above).
2. Practice Drill 1, Pressing Your Buoy (see Chapter 8 for details on this and all drills), for 5–6 minutes of easy 25-yard repeats, resting 10–30 seconds after each repeat. Focus on feeling like more of your body's weight is supported by the water. "Play" with your balance, experimenting with different amounts of pressure. Continue until you feel stable and relaxed for most of each lap.
3. Alternate 25 yards of Drill 1 with 25 yards of SSP-DH (see Chapter 7 for details on this and all sensory skill practice). Practice for 5–6 minutes of easy 25-yard repeats as above until you feel as balanced while swimming as you do drilling. How will you know? You'll feel like you're skimming the surface, hips light and legs relaxed.
4. Alternate 25 yards of swimming SSP-DH with 25 yards of swim-ming (count your strokes), holding your stroke count at -1 s/l. Odd

lengths focus on the downhill part; on even lengths, test your efficiency. Practice for 5–6 minutes of easy 25-yard repeats, resting about
10 seconds between 25s.

5. Practice Drill 3, Rolling to Breathe, as in #2 above. Lead with your
hips (head moves last) and keep your buoy pressure steady at all points
as you roll from front to back and back to front.

6. Alternate 25 yards of Drill 3 with 25 yards of SSP-DH, as in #3
above. As you roll gently, imagine your buoy pressure traveling across
your chest from armpit to armpit rather than as a single point. Keep
hips relaxed (*release* them, don't *hold* them up) and they'll move more
freely.

7. Finish up by repeating #4 above, with new emphasis on gentle roll
and buoy pressure that travels across your whole chest as your body
rolls easily and naturally.

> Note: More experienced swimmers can use 50- or 100-yard repeats or
> even nonstop 5–6-minute swims. Just make sure form is good and
> concentration stays high.

Skill-Builder 2: Make Your Body Longer

1. Warmup (see note on page 260).
2. Practice Drill 5, Single-Arm, for 5–6 minutes of easy 50-yard repeats (25 right arm, 25 left arm), resting 10–20 seconds between each
repeat. Focus first on rolling until your belly button faces the sidewall,
then on having your head, torso, and hips move as one ("head and
butt together"), concentrating about 3 minutes on each.
3. Alternate 25 yards of Drill 5 with 25 yards of SSP-RW for 5–6
minutes as above. On your drill length, focus on pressing your head
and buoy as you roll and on the feeling of having a weightless arm

stretching toward the far wall as you roll. On your swim length, focus on the feeling of reaching s-l-o-w-l-y (as if for something just out of reach on a high shelf) before you stroke.

4. Repeat rounds of 100 yards (25 right arm, 25 left arm, 25 catchup [see drill 6 on page 123 for details], and 25 swim) for 8–10 minutes. Rest after each 25 for 5–10 seconds per length swum. On right arm and left arm, focus on belly button to wall. On catchup, it's head and butt together. On swim, count strokes. Try to hold that count or even shave a stroke here and there if you can.

5. Alternate 25 yards of SSP-RW with 25 yards of swim-and-count-strokes for 5–6 minutes.

6. Finish up with 200 to 300 yards of continuous swimming. Count your strokes on each length and test your ability to maintain a consistent stroke count from beginning to end. If difference between laps with lowest s/l and highest s/l is no greater than 2 strokes, pat yourself on the back.

Skill-Builder 3: Swimming Like a Fish—on Your Side

1. Warmup (see note on page 260).

2. Repeat rounds of 100 yards (25 right arm, 25 left arm, 25 catchup, 25 swim) for 8–10 minutes. Rest after each 25 for 5–10 seconds per length swum. On right arm and left arm, focus on belly button to wall. On catchup, move head and butt together. On swim, count strokes. Shave 1 or 2 s/l if you can on subsequent repetitions.

3. Practice Drill 7, Slide on Your Side, for 5–6 minutes. Alternate 25 yards on your left side with 25 yards on your right. Focus on pressing your head and buoy into the water until you feel easily balanced and relaxed in the side-lying position. You can roll a bit more toward your back if it allows you to breathe more comfortably. Fins may also be a big help.

4. Practice Drill 8, Slide-Front-Slide, for 5–6 minutes or until you're comfortable with staying balanced as you bring one hand up your side to the catchup position and change sides. Rest 5–10 seconds at each wall.

5. Practice Drill 9, Three-Count Slide & Glide, for 5–6 minutes. Rest 5–10 seconds at each wall. Focus on maintaining comfortable balance in each of three positions—lying on your left side, prone catchup position, and lying on your right side—as you count a deliberate "one thousand and one, one thousand and two, one thousand and three" in each.

6. Alternate 25 yards of Drill 9 with 25 yards of swim, resting 5–10 seconds at each wall, for 8–10 minutes. On swim length, cycle through SSP-DH (lap 2), SSP-RW (lap 4) and count your strokes (lap 6), then repeat the pattern until your time is up.

7. Finish up with 200 to 300 yards of continuous swimming. Count your strokes on each length and test your ability to maintain a consistent count from beginning to end. Try to limit difference between lowest s/l and highest s/l to 1 stroke.

Skill-Builder 4: Consolidating Your Efficiency

1. Warmup (see note on page 260).

2. Repeat rounds of 100 yards (25 right arm, 25 left arm, 25 catchup [see Chapter 8 for drill details], 25 swim) for 8–10 minutes. Rest after each 25 for 5–10 seconds/length swum. Count strokes for each length. On right arm, left arm, and catchup, aim for 8–10 strokes each length. On swim, aim for 1 less than your normal stroke count.

3. Swim 50-yard repeats for 10 minutes, resting 15–30 seconds between repeats. Count your strokes for each 50, aiming to hold a consistent stroke count for *all* repeats.

4. Alternate 25 yards of Drill 9 (Three-Count Slide & Glide) with 25 yards of swim for 8–10 minutes. On drill length, practice as in #5 in Skill-Builder #3 above. On swim length, cycle through SSP-DH (lap 2),

SSP-RW (lap 4) and count-your-strokes (lap 6). Then repeat the pattern until time is up.

5. Swim 50-yard swimming golf (see Chapter 7) repeats for 10 minutes, resting just long enough between repeats to calculate your score. Aim to hold a consistent score or improve it slightly during the course of the set.

Skill-Builder 5: Getting the Feel for Effective Swimming

1. Warmup (see note on page 260).
2. Swim 50-yard SSP repeats for 10–12 minutes, resting 15–30 seconds between repeats, as follows: Cycle through 50 yards of DH, 50 of RW, and 50 of WA for duration of set. Focus, focus, focus. Shut out all distractions except the sensation you're looking for. How does your body respond as you change the emphasis slightly on each 50?
3. Swim 50-yard repeats (25 SSP, 25 count-your-strokes) for 5–6 minutes, resting 15–30 seconds between repeats. Use the SSP form that felt best in #2 on the first 25 of each repeat. Try for your best stroke count on the second 25 of each.
4. Swim 50-yard repeats (counting your strokes) for 10–12 minutes, resting 15–30 seconds between repeats. Double your best 25-yard stroke count from #3 above, and aim to keep your 50-yard count within two strokes of that number throughout this set.
5. And now, a little speedwork: swim 25-yard repeats for 5–6 minutes, resting 20–30 seconds between repeats. Swim at a brisk pace (90 percent of your maximum speed) but make sure you complete each 25 within 2 strokes of your count in #3.
6. Finish up with 200 to 300 yards of continuous swimming. Count your strokes on each length and try to hold the count to within 1–2 s/l of #3.

Skill-Builder 6: Introduction to Advanced Drills and Skills

1. Warmup (see note on page 260).
2. Practice 50-yard repeats of Drill 9, Three-Count Slide & Glide, for 5–6 minutes. On first 25 of each, focus on perfect balance in all 3 positions. On second 25 of each, concentrate on creating more surge with stronger hip snap (see Drill 10, Power Surge & Slide).
3. Practice 100-yard repeats for 10–12 minutes. Each repeat is 25 Drill 9, 25 SSP-WA, 25 Drill 10, 25 SSP-HR.
4. Practice Drill 11, Slide on Your Side, for 5–6 minutes of 25-yard repeats, resting 10–15 seconds at each wall. Alternate 25 yards on your right side and 25 on your left.
5. Practice Drill 12, Advanced Slide & Glide, for 5–6 minutes of 25-yard repeats, resting 10 seconds at each wall. Practice until you've mastered pausing on your side, pausing with your head turned down, and swapping hands in front of your head as you switch sides.
6. Practice 50-yard repeats (25 Drill 12, 25 SSP-HS) for 5–6 minutes. Learn to distinguish between the timing of hand-swapping while you swim (SSP) and the timing of switching your hands in front of your head on the drill.
7. Practice 50-yard repeats (25 SSP-HS, 25 count-your-strokes). Continue working on your sense of when to swap your hands in front of your head as you test how this affects your stroke count.

Intermediate Practices

Skill-Builder practices help you master the right movements. Intermediate practices put them to work. They join the principles of Total Immersion swimming with the more conventional training using sets and intervals. But you never completely stop the skill-building, as you'll see. Feel free to modify rest intervals, distances, and number of repeats to make the sessions harder or easier. My suggestions will work best for swimmers who are new to Masters swimming or triathlons and need not just better form but a more challenging and ambitious fitness program.

Intermediate Practice 1
Total: 1,900 yards

1. Warmup (see note on page 260).
2. 3 x 100 @ :20 RI (25 each RA, LA, CU, swim)
Count s/l each length.
3. 4 x 50 @ :15 RI (25 S&G, 25 swim at -1 s/l)
On swim length, swim easy with emphasis on holding at least -1 s/l. (If you normally swim 19 s/l, try to hold to no more than 18 s/l on second length of each 50.)
4. 8 x 25 @ :20 RI fast at -1 sl
Swim as fast as possible, but hold the same s/l established on set #2. Don't take more strokes in order to go faster. Squeeze as much speed out of that stroke count as you can.
5. Main Set: Swim 3 x (200 + 4 x 25 drill EZ)
For the 200s, hold #1 at -2 s/l, #2 at -1 s/l, and #3 at regular s/l. But swim faster on each one. It won't be easy to hold the specified s/l. You may have to kick and glide a little at the end of some lengths.

Note your time for each 200. As you add 1 s/l on each, you should swim a bit faster, so the set emphasizes both stroke efficiency and natural speed building.

Rather than a "passive" rest interval at the wall, use the 25s for "active recovery." Choose a drill for 25 yards and rest 5–10 seconds at end of each. After the fourth 25, start your next 200 on the next "top" (0 integer on pace clock.)

6. 4 x 50 cooldown: 25 EZ back, 25 EZ breast
Count s/l on each.

Intermediate Practice 2
Total: 1,900 yards

1. Warmup (see note on page 260).
2. SSP set. 2 x **25** DH @ :10 RI
     50 25 DH, 25 WA @ :15 RI
     75 25 DH, 25 WA, 25 RW @ :20 RI
     100 25 DH, 25 WA, 25 RW, 25 HS @ :30 RI

This set focuses completely on the sensory experience, training the nervous system to become more and more comfortable with efficient movements. Ignore the clock (except for tracking your rest intervals). You can even skip stroke counting, if that's distracting to you.

3. Main set: 6 x 100 @ :30 RI
Hold s/l constant.

Your challenge is to maintain s/l as you swim farther. For an additional challenge, try to hold time constant too. Repeat this set periodically—adding repeats or decreasing rest—as your "efficiency endurance" increases.

4. 4 x 75 (25 ASG, 25 RW, 25 HS) @ :30–:40 RI
The drill on the first length of each 75 acts as a setup for the SSP practice on the next 2 lengths.

5. Cooldown: 200 EZ free/back
Cycle through 25 free and 25 back to loosen up.

Appendix — — — — — — — — — — — — —

Intermediate Practice 3
Total: 2,000 yards

1. Warmup (see note on page 260).
2. 5 x 100 (50 SSP-SH, 50 count-your-strokes) @ :20 RI
   On the first 50 of every 100, make sure your hands pull back no faster than your body is moving forward. Hold s/l constant on second 50 of each 100 throughout the set.
3. 2 rounds of 5 x 50 @ :30 RI, swimming golf
   Goal is to lower your swimming golf score (strokes + seconds) in 2 sets of 5 x 50. You'll end up with a total of 10 "rounds of golf" and 10 scores. If you need more than 30 seconds to figure your score, go ahead and take more time between 50s. On first round, try to hold time and reduce s/l. On 2nd round, try to hold s/l and reduce time.
4. 500 fartlek (25 EZ back, 25 free, 25 EZ breast, 25 free)
   Count strokes on back and breast (stretch yourself out) and hold a brisk pace on freestyle lengths.
5. Cooldown: 4 x 50 drill or SSP, your choice, @ :20 RI

Intermediate Practice 4
Total: 1,800 yards

1. Warmup (see note on page 260).
2. 3 rounds of (1 x 100 drill @:20 RI + 2 x 50 count @:10 RI)
   Choose one drill for the whole set or change to a new drill in each round. On 50s swim, try to reduce count by 1 s/l on each successive round.
3. 2 rounds of (2 x 50 with fists closed + 2 x 50 swim + 2 x 50 with paddles)
   Rest :10—:15 between all 50s. Reduce count by 1 s/l from fists set to swim set and from swim set to paddles set.

Appendix

4. Cooldown: 1 x 300 (4 x 25 S&G-3, 25 SSP-RW, 25 ASG, 25 SSP-HS)
   Odd 25s are drill; even 25s are SSP.

Intermediate Practice 5
Total: 2,000 yards

1. Warmup (see note on page 260).
2. 3 x 100 (50 drill, 50 swim at -2 s/l) @ :30 RI
   Choose 1 drill for whole set, or change drills each 100. 50 swim (stroke eliminator at -2 s/l) must be superefficient. Gets you ready for the next set.
3. Swim 4 x 100 (build by 50s) @ 1:00 RI
   On each 100, start with an EZ 50 at -1 s/l, then a faster 50 at normal s/l.
4. Swim 3 x 100 @ :20 RI. Hold -1 s/l & descend
   100 drill (your choice)
   Swim 3 x 100 @ :40 RI. Hold normal s/l and descend
   The challenge in this item is to hold your s/l count consistent while descending within each set. On the second set, your times should be a bit faster than on the first because you have more strokes to work with.
5. Cooldown: 6 x 50 golf @ :20 RI

Intermediate Practice 6
Total: 2,000 yards

1. Warmup (see note on page 260).
2. 200 drill (your choice) + 2 x 100 SSP (your choice) + 4 x 50 swim at -1 s/l
   Rest :20 after each item in this set

3. Swim 6 x 100 @ :20 RI. Odd 100s SSP; Even 100s descend.

Numbers 1-3-5 are SSP (50 DH, 50 HS); numbers 2-4-6 are count at -1 s/l. Try to descend while holding the stroke count constant.

4. 6 x 50 @ :15 RI. Descend even 50s.

This set of 50s follows the same pattern as the 100s in preceding set. Numbers 1-3-5 are SSP-RW; numbers 2-4-6 are count at -1 s/l. Try to descend while holding the stroke count constant.

5. Cooldown: 200 EZ, choice of stroke, drill, or SSP.

Veteran Practices

If you're an experienced swimmer—perhaps you've competed on an age-group or school team or are already training regularly with a Masters swim team—you're probably ready to dive into these practices. They're longer and a little more complex than the Intermediate practices, but as they bring the aerobic system to a high level of conditioning, they also still work on all the Total Immersion principles of purposeful laps that groom the nervous system to make efficiency a habit. If they sound like top-of-the-line training, it may be because these practices are from my own log. They're how I get ready for Masters competition in events from 100 to 1,650 yards or 1,500 meters. Feel free to modify rest intervals, distances, or number of repeats to make them a little tougher or a little easier for you.

Veteran Practice 1
Total: 3,200 yards

1. Warmup (see note on page 260).
2. 3 rounds of (4 x 100 swim + 8 x 25 drill EZ @ :10 RI)
   First round: 100s @ :20 RI; second round: 100s @ :15 RI; third

round: 100s @ :10 RI. The challenge in this set is to hold a steady pace on all 3 rounds of 4 x 100 as rest decreases. Use the 25s with your choice of stroke drill to recover. For an extra challenge, try to hold your s/l even as you reduce your rest intervals on the second and third rounds of 4 x 100. Rest 1:00 extra between rounds.

3. 4 rounds of 4 x 50 @ :15 RI
    #1: 25 CU, 25 count
    #2: 25 S&G-3, 25 count
    #3: 25 ASG, 25 count
    #4: 50 count & descend (swimming golf)

4. Cooldown: 200 EZ (25 back, 25 breast)

Veteran Practice 2
Total: 3,600 yards

1. Warmup (see note on page 260).
2. Swim 2 rounds of 3 x 200 @ 1:00 RI EZ back/brisk free mix

In each round, first 200 is 100 back, 100 free, second 200 is 2 x (50 back, 50 free), third 200 is 4 x (25 back, 25 free). All backstroke is EZ with emphasis on hip rotation rhythms. This serves as "active rest" for brisk-pace freestyle. Freestyle pace/length should increase as distance swum drops from 100 to 50 to 25 yards. In other words, the 4 x 25 free in the third 200 should be at a faster pace than the 1 x 100 free in the first 200. Rest 1:00 extra between rounds.

3. 3 rounds of (4 x 100 EZ drill @ :20 RI + 8 x 25 fast @ :30 RI)

This set reverses the pattern on set #2 in Veteran Practice 1 above, putting emphasis on speed rather than pace. In each round the 4 x 100 is recovery and emphasizes stroke efficiency. The 8 x 25 should be swum fast, but maintain s/l count at no more than +1 s/l.

4. Cooldown: 4 x 50 golf @ :20 RI

Veteran practice 3
Total: 3,200 yards

1. Warmup (see note on page 260).
2. 8 x 75 @ :20 RI (25 Slide on Side, 25 S&G-3, 25 count)
3. Swim 8 x 50 @ :10 RI + 4 x 25 EZ @ :10 RI +
      4 x 100 @ :20 RI + 4 x 25 EZ @ :10 RI +
      2 x 200 @ :30 RI + 4 x 25 EZ @ :10 RI +
      1 x 400 @ :40 RI + 4 x 25 EZ @ :10 RI

This can be approached in two ways. The left half is your challenge; the right half is your recovery. The challenge can be to maintain s/l count as repeat distances increase or to maintain pace/length as distances increase (i.e., swim each 50 very comfortably in :45, then try to swim each 100 in 1:30, each 200 in 3:00, and the 400 in 6:00 or better). EZ 25s can be choice of drill, SSP, or counting s/l.

4. Cooldown: 4 x 50 count at -2 s/l @ :15 RI

Veteran practice 4
Total: 3,000 yards

1. Warmup (see note on page 260).
2. 200 back (25 kick, 25 swim), 200 free (25 kick, 25 swim), 200 (25 free, 25 back SSP-HR).

Do all kicking on side; emphasize hip roll on all swimming, both free and back. Do this as a straight 600.

3. 4 x 50 @ :15 RI 25 CU, 25 swim & count
   1 x 50 @ :15 RI swim & count
   1 x 300 @ :60 RI swim & count
   4 x 50 @ :15 RI 25 S&G-3, 25 swim & count
   2 x 25 @ :10 RI swim & count
   2 x 150 @ :30 RI swim & count

On the 300, you get to take only as many s/l as on the 1 x 50. On the 150s, take only as many s/l as on the 2 x 25, then kick on side to wall if you run out of strokes and haven't reached the wall.

4. 3 rounds of 4 x 50. Count strokes and take time (swimming golf).

Round 1: #s1–4 @ :20 RI

Round 2: #s5–8 @ :15 RI

Round 3: #s9–12 @ :10 RI

Your stroke count may increase as your interval decreases. Your goal is to maintain same stroke count and time throughout the set. If unable to hold both the same, repeat the set every couple of weeks until you can.

5. 300 cooldown: (25 kick, 25 back, 25 kick, 25 free). All kick on side.

Veteran practice 5
Total: 3,200 yards

1. Warmup (see note on page 260).
2. SSP Set: 4 rounds of 25 DH @ :10 RI

50 DH-WA @ :15 RI

75 DH-WA-HS @ :20 RI

100 DH-WA-HS-BB @ :30 RI

This is mainly a test of concentration and your ability to quickly switch gears on your SSP as you add another length and an additional SSP object to each repeat. At the conclusion of each round, start again at the top on the next round or reverse the order on the even rounds and go 100–75–50–25.

3. Main Set: 4 x 300 swim @ :30 RI

#s 1 & 3 maintain count of -1 s/l

#s 2 & 4 brisk pace and count s/l

On the odd 300s, you'll focus exclusively on maximum stroke efficiency. On the even 300s, swim at a brisk pace while monitoring your stroke count to see how many extra s/l it adds. See if you can hold your s/l closer to maximum efficiency on #4 than you did on #2.

4. 200 choice of drill EZ, 8 x 25 fast @ :20 RI, 200 choice of SSP EZ

Combination of recovery, speedwork, and final cooldown. Try to reduce s/l by 1 stroke on second 4 of 8 x 25, yet hold speed the same.

Veteran Practice 6
Total: 4,000 yards

1. Warmup (see note on page 260).
2. 4 x 50 @ :15 RI 25 drill, 25 count -1 s/l
   3 x 100 swim @ :30 RI count -1 s/l
   4 x 50 @ :15 RI 25 drill, 25 count -1 s/l
   2 x 150 swim @ :40 RI count -1 s/l
   4 x 50 @ :15 RI 25 drill, 25 count -1s/l
   1 x 300 swim count -1s/l

This set is a challenge to hold stroke efficiency at increasing distances. The 4 x 50 drill-swim set is a setup to hone stroke efficiency, which is then tested on the 300-yard swim sets. It will be harder to hold stroke count on the 150s than on the 100s and harder still on the 300.

3. 8 x 25 swim @ :20 RI. Swim fast but hold s/l at -1.
   8 x 25 swim @ :30 RI. Swim faster but hold normal s/l.
4. Repeat set #2 but with s/l at normal count.

Same challenge as in the earlier set, but swims should be faster as you can add 1 s/l to count from the earlier set.

5. Cooldown: 200 EZ (25 back, 25 breast)

WHERE TO GO FOR WHAT:
YOUR DIRECTORY TO RESOURCES FOR BETTER
TOTAL IMMERSION SWIMMING

Swimming and Triathlon Magazines and Publications

Fitness Swimmer. A Rodale Press publication, targeted at casual through serious fitness swimmers. Published four times yearly; will publish six times annually starting in 1997. Newsstand: $2.95/issue. Six-issue subscription: $19.95. Phone: (800)846-0086.

Swim. All members of Masters swimming receive six issues per year as part of their membership, but non-Masters swimmers can also find articles of interest and may subscribe without joining Masters swimming. Bimonthly. Newsstand: $3.95/issue. One-year subscription: $19.95. Phone: (800)352-7946.

Swimming Technique. A serious journal targeted at swim coaches and researchers. Technical information may interest the extremely serious Masters swimmer but probably won't be much help to the casual fitness swimmer. Quarterly. One-year subscription: $13.00. Phone: (800)352-7946.

Swimming World. The bible of competitive swimming. Most articles are for and about competitive swimmers ages eight-and-under through college. Monthly. Newsstand: $2.50/issue. One-year subscription: $19.00. Phone: (800)352-7946.

Places to Swim

Swimmers' Guide (American Lap Swimmers Association, updated yearly), 349 pages. Lists over 3,000 year-round locations, including municipal, Y, school, health club, and hotel pools in 1,700 U.S. cities, for traveling swimmers. Provides hours of availability, admissions policies and fees, addresses, telephone numbers, dimensions, and water temperatures. Available for $15.95 from Total Immersion. Phone: (800)609-7946.

Information Sources

For Information About Masters Swimming:

U.S. Masters Swimming, Inc. (USMS)
Dorothy Donnelly, Secretary
2 Peter Avenue
Rutland, MA 01543
Phone: (508)886-6631, Fax: (508)886-6265
Dorothy Donnelly will tell you how to reach local contacts and registrars for Masters swimming in your area. The local contact can tell you the locations of coached Masters programs and pools with lap hours.

For Information About Age-Group, Open, and
Olympic Competitive Swimming:

International Swimming Hall of Fame
One Hall of Fame Drive
Fort Lauderdale, FL 33316
Phone: (305)462-6536

United States Swimming, Inc. (USS)
One Olympic Plaza
Colorado Springs, CO 80909
Phone: (719)578-4578, Fax: (719)578-4669

For Information About Total Immersion Workshops and Videos and Any of the "Pool Tools" Recommended in This Book:

Total Immersion, Inc.
119 W. Main Street
Goshen, NY 10924
Phone: (800)609-7946
E-mail: Totalswimm@aol.com

The Total Immersion stroke improvement drill progression in Chapter 8 is also illustrated on a 30-minute video. This video, focusing on freestyle technique as taught by Terry Laughlin at his weekend workshops, includes each of his drills with all critical aspects highlighted in slow-motion and stop action, viewed from both above and under the water. The drills are presented in the same sequence as they are at the workshop with all the verbal cues and reminders used by Terry as he teaches. The video is available for $39.95. Subsequent videos will cover skill-drill-based learning sequences for backstroke, breaststroke, and butterfly, also taught using Total Immersion principles, and a video of dry-land strength and flexibility exercise for swimmers.

Total Immersion has also produced a spiral-bound, waterproof flipchart of all stroke drills for poolside reference as you practice. The flipchart is available for $19.95.

INDEX

Abduction, shoulder, 234
Aerobic training, 69, 150–53, 156,
    170, 171
  in intervals, 177
  for middle distance racing,
    188
  training nervous system versus,
    66, 67
  weight control and, 212
Aging, 147–48, 185
  flexibility and, 229
  muscle loss and, 219–20
American College of Sports
    Medicine, 215–16, 220
American Statistical Association,
    210
American Swimming Coaches
    Association, 14
America's Cup, 50
Anaerobic training, 151–53, 155,
    156, 165, 166, 170, 171
  in intervals, 177, 184
  for middle distance races, 188
  for sprints, 187
Ankle flexibility, 86
  speed and, 197
  vertical kicking for, 118
Ankle straps, 195
Arms
  lengthening and, 120–26
  propulsion and, 57–60
  strengthening, on swim bench,
    201

weight training and, 220
weightless, 48–49, 94, 96, 127,
    128, 229
Arthur, Ransom, 237

Back, balancing on, 113–14
Backstroke, 162
  in races, 244
Balance, 40–44, 65
  injury prevention and, 229
  kick and, 85, 196–97
  lengthening and, 119–26
  pull buoys and, 199
  in sensory skill practice, 95
  in side-lying position, 53, 128–39
  skill drills for, 77, 110–17
Barry, Betty, 245
Basic fitness, 154
  consistency to achieve, 160
Benches, swim, 201–2
Bell, Keith, 253
Biceps curls, 233
Bike riding, *see* Cycling
Biondi, Matt, 66–67, 81, 159, 186
Birch, Beryl Bender, 232
Bite-size movements, 15, 68, 82
Bladed fins, 86, 197–98
Body position, 15, 27
  sensory skill practice and, 92–93
  see also Side-lying position
Body-streamlining, *see* Drag,
    reducing
Bodyweight exercises, 220–25

Index — — — — — — — — — — — — — — —